'David Hulme's is a passiona[te] plea for attacking poverty r[ather than] washing ashore in the Me[diterranean] about definitions of poverty [and inequality], but it is no longer possible in our interconnected planet to deny the self-interests of the wealthy West in addressing pandemics, narco-trafficking, climate deterioration and terrorism. Read why things have to change.'

Thomas G. Weiss, The CUNY Graduate Center

'This excellent short book provides a succinct overview of current debates on foreign aid, and argues that it is not aid itself which should be at issue, but its form and content. Marshalling a wide literature, it proposes a pivot towards new horizons such as trade and the environment. The argument is developed in a form which will be accessible to a broad range of readers, including civil society and policy makers.'

Ravi Kanbur, Charles H. Dyson School of
Applied Economics and Management, Cornell University

'We live in "one world": this book provides a powerful and accessible exposition of what this means for ethics, policies and politics.'

Frances Stewart, University of Oxford

'This is a timely and magisterial overview, wide-ranging and judicious, an invaluable update on where we are and where we should go in international development.'

Robert Chambers, Institute of Development Studies

'In an age where nations are highly integrated yet increasingly unequal, there is no more important issue than ensuring that everyone "lives well". But how to achieve this? As Hulme carefully argues, old paradigms focused on conditional aid to political allies but indifference to domestic politics must give way to a focus on how relations between and within nations – rich, rising and failing alike – are structured. Everyday citizens and development professionals around the world need to grapple with these issues, and in Hulme they have both a passionate and an instructive guide.'

Michael Woolcock, World Bank and Harvard University

'A timely book on global poverty that is not about poverty but about why we should ALL care for it. The globalized economy of the 21st century needs a normative basis for global partnerships for sustainable development.'

Sakiko Fukuda-Parr, The New School, New York

Should Rich Nations Help the Poor?

Global Futures Series

David Hulme

Should Rich Nations Help the Poor?

polity

First published in 2016 by Polity Press

Polity Press
65 Bridge Street
Cambridge CB2 1UR, UK

Polity Press
350 Main Street
Malden, MA 02148, USA

ISBN-13: 978-0-7456-8605-9
ISBN-13: 978-0-7456-8606-6 (pb)

A catalogue record for this book is available from the British Library.

Names: Hulme, David, author.
Title: Should rich nations help the poor? / David Hulme.
Description: Cambridge, UK ; Malden, MA : Polity Press, 2016. | Includes
    bibliographical references.
Identifiers: LCCN 2015047855 (print) | LCCN 2016004750 (ebook) |
    ISBN 9780745686059 (hardback) | ISBN 9780745686066 (pbk.) | ISBN
    9780745686080 (Mobi) | ISBN 9780745686097 (Epub)
Subjects: LCSH: Economic assistance--Moral and ethical aspects--Developing
    countries. | Economic development--Moral and ethical aspects--Developing
    countries. | Developed countries--Foreign economic relations--Developing
    countries. | Developing countries--Foreign economic relations--Developed
    countries.
Classification: LCC HC60 .H866155 2016 (print) | LCC HC60 (ebook) | DDC
    338.9109172/4--dc23
LC record available at http://lccn.loc.gov/2015047855

Typeset in 11 on 15 Sabon by
Servis Filmsetting Ltd, Stockport, Cheshire
Printed and bound in the United Kingdom by Clays Ltd, St Ives PLC

For further information on Polity, visit our website: politybooks.com

Contents

Acknowledgements

My academic colleagues and students at the University of Manchester's Global Development Institute (GDI; previously known as the Institute for Development Policy and Management and Brooks World Poverty Institute) have provided the intellectual base and academic stimulation behind this essay. My particular thanks to colleagues who read full drafts of the manuscript and provided invaluable advice: Tony Bebbington, Dan Brockington, Chris Jordan and Sophie King. Also thanks to colleagues who provided specialist guidance on the analysis: Nicola Banks, Armando Barrientos, Admos Chimhowu, Sam Hickey, Heiner Janus, Uma Kothari, Fabiola Mieres, James Scott, Kunal Sen, Rorden Wilkinson and Pablo Yanguas-gil. Comments and advice from doctoral students at GDI's 'Work-in-Progress' seminars were very help-

Acknowledgements

ful. My personal assistant at the GDI, Denise Redston, did a million jobs (as usual) that permitted the volume to be completed – many thanks, again.

I am indebted to Louise Knight at Polity Press, who had the original idea for the book, provided excellent guidance and thoughtful comments throughout, and whose energy motivated me from its inception to its completion. Louise's colleagues at Polity, Nekane Tanaka Galdos and Pascal Porcheron, supported me through submission and production. Justin Dyer helped edit the text into a form much more readable than the original.

Last, but not least, sincere thanks to the countless people – from heads of UN agencies to NGO field-workers in Tanzania to poor women in the villages of Bangladesh – who have helped me understand, over the years, what it means to live in 'one world'.

1

Why Worry About the Distant Poor?

Rich nations, and their citizens, are increasingly experiencing the consequences of living in a very unequal world. Much of this is to their advantage: cheap garden furniture from China, fashionable, low-cost clothing from Bangladesh and affordable petrol. But there is also a downside. Holidaymakers from Northern Europe are keeping away from some Mediterranean beaches as it spoils your fun when the bodies of refugees wash up. There are deep tensions in mainland Europe about the growing flows of migrants and refugees. These stretch from the west, where Britain and France have been at loggerheads about migrant camps around Calais, to the east, where EU and non-EU countries are erecting new iron curtains. Meanwhile, the last time I travelled from Mexico to the US, the queue to pass through the Tijuana border control snaked back more than a mile. Having so much poverty and inequality in an affluent world means that rich nations and their citizens have no choice but to think through how they relate to the distant poor.

Extreme poverty has reduced greatly in recent years, but poverty is a long way from eradication. Almost 3 billion people are deprived of at least one basic human need: lack of access to food, drinking water, shelter, basic health services, not to mention education – and dignity. Some 800 million people went to sleep hungry last night, and one billion experienced the indignity of having to defecate in the open. Even more shocking, 19,000 children will die today of easily preventable causes: one unnecessary child death every five seconds all day every day.

Our grandparents, and perhaps our parents, could accept such conditions. They believed that there were just not enough resources (and technology and organization) to provide for every human being. But we cannot use this excuse today – we live in an affluent world. Our agricultural systems produce enough food to feed all 7 billion of us. Low-cost medicines, basic health services and simple health practices (washing hands after using the toilet and sleeping under a mosquito net) would save millions of human lives every year. A reallocation of a mere

1% of global income to the poorest would entirely eradicate US$1.90-a-day income poverty.[1]

How is it that avoidable human suffering and preventable deaths occur on such a vast scale after 25 years of unprecedented global economic wealth creation? Newspaper headlines and media coverage create the impression that extreme poverty and destitution are caused by emergencies and disasters. These are both man-made and natural, ranging from violent conflict in Syria to hurricanes in the Caribbean, floods in Africa and earthquakes in Asia. But these humanitarian crises are only a part of the story. More thoughtful analyses find that the main causes are grounded in less dramatic, more mundane processes: low wages; lack of access to productivity-enhancing agricultural technologies; indebtedness to moneylenders; the profit margins and business models that corporations pursue; the investment decisions (and bonuses) that bankers take; poor-quality basic services; and the public policies that governments select and implement – or fail to implement.

From an early age I understood that there were very different ideas about how rich nations and better-off people could try to help poor people in faraway places. In the mid-1960s, from the relative comfort of a council house near Liverpool, my parents had very different responses when the BBC reported that India 'faced famine'. My mother thought the UK government 'should send them food': if people were starving, then others with food should spare them some. By contrast, my father thought 'they should all be sterilized'. The Indian government should do this, and should not be over-concerned about whether sterilization was voluntary. The UK government could assist the Indian authorities with finance and medical expertise. 'Over-population', not access to food, was the underlying problem.

Fifty years later, such contrasting positions are still argued out – not by my parents, but in the media. Charity fundraising advertisements on television encourage donations for poor children in poor countries. The BBC's Children in Need programme goes beyond this focus on charity. It also reports on successful UK government aid projects that help girls complete primary and secondary schooling across Asia and avoid female genital mutilation in Africa. The message is clear: relatively small amounts of money can make a big difference at household and community levels. Less clear, but implicitly: isn't it your moral duty (and your government's) to help those who are poor? A contrasting position comes from the right-wing news media like Fox News in the US and the *Daily Mail* in the UK. These present aid programmes as inefficient and highlight that corruption in recipient countries means that aid money is 'wasted'. Explicitly, they argue there is next to nothing that better-off outsiders can do to help poor people in poor countries beyond humanitarian work. Implicitly, they suggest that it is 'not our job' to provide help. Poor countries and poor people need to sort themselves out.

In this book I explore these contrasting viewpoints and ask: 'Should rich nations help the poor?' I argue that rich nations should help the governments and people of poor countries to achieve prosperity and human development. But the argument goes further: those of us who are 'better-off' would be stupid not to help the poor. Not only is this the morally right thing to do, but the pursuit of self-interest, indeed the future well-being of rich world citizens (our children and grandchildren), requires that we help poor people in faraway lands.

Migration, the focus of the opening paragraph, is not the only issue that makes global poverty and inequality topical in rich countries. The Ebola virus illustrates this vividly. In 2014, Ebola caused devastation across parts of West Africa, and health authorities across Europe, North America, China and Japan made detailed plans about how they would respond to the arrival of the disease – especially if the nightmare scenario occurred and it mutated into airborne transmission. But the rich world's response to West Africa's problem was tardy. This disease has been known about for decades, but research on medicines to prevent or treat it has been very limited: it only kills poor Africans, so who would pay for research? A similarly sluggish response to an emerging health problem in Africa 30 years ago permitted HIV/AIDS to become a global pandemic, killing millions in Europe, the US and other rich countries. And now we have the Zika virus.

Have we learned nothing? On a small, densely populated, highly connected planet a problem in a faraway place can soon become a problem anywhere. Unexpected population movements and health are not the only examples of our interconnectedness. Desperately poor people in Latin America opt to grow and/or transport cocaine to the US as the economic opportunities they have offer few alternatives. As a result, large parts of Central America have been destabilized and the chains of narco-violence spill over into US cities. In the Middle East, religious ideologies take root that legitimate violence and terrorism at home and abroad. The question we need to ask is not simply

Why Worry About the Distant Poor?

'Should rich nations help the poor?' but 'What are the best ways for rich nations to help the poor?'

Why things have to change

There are three main reasons why rich country support for the distant poor cannot go on the way it is today. First, it is not working: the underpinning idea that a set of developed countries can help a set of developing countries to 'catch up' is now untenable. Countries that were once classed as developing – Chile, Mexico and South Korea – are now members of the OECD, the club of rich nations. A whole set of others are holding talks about joining the OECD (Colombia, Costa Rica, Malaysia and Peru). Brazil, China and India are all recognized as emerging powers and have been running their own aid programmes (being donors) at the same time as they have been recipients of aid. The world is a complex multi-polar mosaic and not a Global North that needs to help a Global South.

Second, the idea that development can be achieved largely through foreign aid (government-to-government financial transfers) has been discredited. Countries that have experienced significant improvements in the well-being of their population in recent years have achieved this through engaging with markets/international trade and selectively participating in a set of processes commonly described as 'globalization'. Interactions between the civil societies of different countries (the women's movement, the environment movement, development and human rights NGOs, faith-based organizations, diaspora communities, etc.) have been an important part of these processes. Nation states remain crucial, but their role is at least as much about enabling development as about delivering development. By contrast, countries that have made little development progress often have high levels of political instability and/or violent conflict. These are commonly referred to as 'fragile states'. In such circumstances the role of rich countries is about working out how to support domestic processes of state formation (getting governments to work more effectively and inclusively) rather than simply transferring foreign aid.

Third, the idea of 'international development' is being totally recast as the evidence grows that countries with large numbers of poor people cannot simply copy what the industrialized countries have done. Sustainable development is now the UN-agreed, global meta-goal. The high levels of carbon emissions that we take for granted in the

West – from our factories, farms, transport and houses – have already created global warming. The material basis of 'development' has to be redefined if the world's population – presently 7 billion but in the not too distant future 8 or 9, perhaps 10 billion – is to survive and have reasonable lives: what some Latin American thinkers are conceptualizing as *buen vivir* (living well). Living well will mean significantly improved material conditions for at least 3 billion poor and very poor people – better access to food, clean water, sanitation, shelter, health services, energy and other goods and services. But it will also have to mean living differently for elites and middle classes around the world (you and I included). The material- and energy-profligate lifestyles that rich nations and better-off people now have cannot continue in a world that is sustainable and socially just. Helping the world's poor is no longer simply about changes in poorer countries: it is also about big changes in rich nations.

Helping the poor: a scorecard

The conventional way of deciding whether rich nations are concerned about people in poorer countries is to look at their foreign aid budgets (official development assistance or ODA). If one does this, then there is evidence that virtually all high-income countries have some concerns, as all allocate public funds for international development. In aggregate terms the US would appear to be the most concerned country, as it spent US$32.7 billion on official development assistance in 2014.[2] However, it has the world's biggest economy, and the more usual measure is share of gross national income (GNI) spent as foreign aid. From this perspective the US comes out as a poor performer, with only 0.19% of its GNI spent on development in other countries, compared to the OECD average of 0.29%. But it beats South Korea, which managed only 0.13%. At the top of the list for aid spending come Sweden (1.10%) and Norway (0.99%). The UK is the most improved, reaching the UN Millennium Development Goal (MDG) target of 0.70% in 2014.

However, foreign aid is only one of the ways in which rich nations can support poor countries and poor people. The Centre for Global Development asks the question 'Which wealthy nations are helping poor ones the most?' and computes a Commitment to Development Index (CDI).[3] This index combines seven different ways in which support can be offered to poor countries:

foreign aid; being open to trade; contributing to a global financial regime that helps ensure that poor countries get access to finance; allowing the citizens of developing countries to immigrate; taking responsibility for environmental impacts; contributing to improved security; and making technologies available to poorer nations. This is not a perfect measure, but it is much better than simply looking at aid levels.

Again, Scandinavian countries head this listing, with Denmark at 6.8 (out of a possible 10), Sweden at 6.6 and Norway at 6.2. The UK comes out as a good performer with a 5.6 score. The US does better than on the simple ODA measure, coming 19 out of 27 rich nations with 4.6. At the bottom end of the ranking come Japan and South Korea. Both score 3.3 out of 10: they do not help poor people in poor countries very much according to this measure.

Doing the right thing – for the wrong reasons

Why do rich nations help the poor in faraway places? There are a mix of very different reasons, ranging from the high-minded – 'It's our moral duty' – to the venal – 'We can look good and make a fast buck out of this'. Commonly, the governments of rich countries use combinations of altruism and self-interest to justify support for the distant needy to their taxpayers. There are four distinct lines of argument.

The most commonly heard reason that the leaders and politicians of rich nations make for supporting the distant needy is moral duty. All human beings should be compassionate and should seek to reduce the suffering of other human beings. In particular, those whose basic needs are secure should assist those who are not so fortunate. This is not simply about helping relatives, friends and neighbours, but, as the distinguished philosopher Peter Singer argues, it applies to all of humanity: '... it makes no moral difference whether the person I help is a neighbor's child ten yards away from me or a Bengali whose name I shall never know, ten thousand miles away.'[4] The pursuit of social justice requires that the poor in any part of the world should be assisted by those individuals (and their governments) with the means to help. From this perspective such actions are not simply charity, they are a duty. How could anyone spend US$5 on a fancy cup of coffee when US$5 could pay for the medicine to save a child's life in Africa?

The second argument, moral responsibility, is based on causal analysis. It holds that the mature, industrial countries – rich nations – and their citizens must support poor nations because they are responsible for the economic and political structures that have made countries and populations poor. In effect, this is a critique of colonialism, post-colonial developmentalism, contemporary capitalism and globalization. It views such processes as a major cause, in some cases *the* cause, of global poverty, global inequality and social injustice. The impacts of colonialism (resource extraction, racism, ethnic divisions, slavery and societal breakdown, illogical national boundaries, government by narrow predatory elites that hold power, etc.) have created historical legacies that continue to impoverish poor nations. The classic example is the North Atlantic slave trade, which depopulated and socially destabilized West Africa in ways that hamper development today. While all colonial powers have left negative legacies, the Belgians are sometimes held up as bequeathing some of the greatest problems, such as fostering an ethnic divide in Rwanda between the revenue-collecting rulers (Tutsi) and the taxpaying ruled (Hutu) that laid the basis for the genocide of 1994.

And so to the present: a manifestly unfair world trade regime helps keep poor people poor. African cotton farmers are impoverished while US cotton farmers receive vast public subsidies to keep them going. The average cow in the EU receives grants of US$2.50 a day: more income than around one-third of humanity. Multinational corporations (MNCs) based in rich countries dominate business in many poorer countries and illicitly help extract US$10 from poor countries for every US$1 of foreign aid the rich world provides.[5] The world's leading pharmaceutical companies, based in Europe and the US, charge such high prices for their products that millions of poor people die unnecessarily. Rich country control over finance and technology ensures that poorer countries cannot compete economically or meet the social needs of their populations. Furthermore, the policies pursued by the IMF and World Bank are tightly monitored by the US government (and thus indirectly by US corporate interests). Such evidence has created heated debates among leading philosophers about whether poor countries have an ethical case to declare a 'just war' against rich nations in order to protect the lives of their citizens![6]

In recent years a further strand of argument, climate change, has greatly strengthened the case that the rich nations are responsible for poverty in low-income nations. The world's most economically advanced countries and wealthiest people have pumped so much CO_2 into the atmosphere that this is now undermining the livelihoods of poor people in poor countries.

The third argument for rich nations helping the poor – common interests – is based as much on self-interest as altruism. It posits that people whose basic needs are met should assist the poor if they want to maintain and improve their own well-being. This applies to neighbours and to non-neighbours. The relatively better-off should assist poor people: to improve local and national social cohesion; to reduce the incentives for excluded social groups to threaten social and economic stability; to create economic opportunities; to reduce the likelihood of public health problems and pandemics; and to reduce rates of migration and population growth.

The arguments about health and migration have been highly evident in recent years. Without effective health policy support from rich nations, the likelihood of major new diseases, such as Ebola, evolving in poor countries and subsequently spreading across the world is much higher. Similarly, any serious attempt to reduce the flow of Africans crossing the Mediterranean to live in Europe (estimated at 200,000 in 2015) entails rich nations actively promoting economic growth and job creation in Africa so that the stark inequality in economic opportunities between the two continents is dramatically reduced. Relatedly, if you want to cap global population at 9 billion, rather than 10 or 11 billion, then you need to reduce poverty rapidly in the poorest parts of the world (especially sub-Saharan Africa).The best way to bring down fertility rates is not to hand out contraceptives but to reduce poverty. Prosperity in Bangladesh has brought the total fertility rate (the average number of births in a lifetime per woman) down from 5.2 to 2.1 in just 30 years.

An important argument in the West has been that if the distant needy have no prospects for improvement, then some of them might be more likely to support violent political groups and/or engage in drug trafficking and international crime. At the extreme they may become terrorists. So, helping the distant needy may not only be 'the right thing to do', it might also reduce the social and political problems rich nations face. This argument has been common in the US since 9/11, although the evidence to support it is very limited. The 9/11 suicide bombers were from Saudi Arabia (a high-income country) and none of them came from impoverished backgrounds. The Daesh[7] terrorists in Paris in 2015 were from middle-class families. The more pertinent argument is that in countries where poverty is the norm, governance is often poor and terrorists can establish bases and training camps there (Afghanistan, Nigeria, Syria and Yemen). There is also a strong liberal economic strand to the common interests argument. The more poor nations and poor people around the world increase their incomes, the greater will be the economic opportunities for wealthier nations and people.

However, behind these three publicly propounded reasons for helping poor countries a fourth and much less noble set of motives has often been uppermost in the thinking of rich nations: short-term political and commercial advantages. Geopolitical considerations were a priority throughout the Cold War, with the US and its allies, and the USSR and its allies, seeking to outmanoeuvre each other through buying the support of poorer countries and their leaders with development and military aid packages. This did not simply mean giving foreign aid to a country. It meant giving foreign aid to murderous dictators, such as President Mobutu of the Democratic Republic of Congo (formerly Zaïre). Wider foreign policy considerations have also shaped the aid allocation practices of rich nations. Lavish aid flows from the US to Egypt and Israel over the decades reflect an interest in supporting friendly states rather than poor people.

Why Worry About the Distant Poor?

Alongside foreign policy considerations are commercial interests. Rich countries have commonly 'tied' their aid to contracts for their home companies and NGOs; allocated aid as export credits for domestic businesses; and used aid as a form of inducement for commercial contracts to be placed with the aid-giving nation. Margaret Thatcher's public humiliation over the Pergau Dam – when her government was successfully taken to court for providing the Malaysian government with increased aid in return for their ordering British armaments – is a classic example of aid pursuing commercial interests.

While the arguments presented above – moral duty, moral responsibility, common interests and self-interest – support the idea of rich nations helping the poor, they have been, and continue to be, fiercely challenged. Recently the case against helping distant strangers has gained support in several countries – Australia, Canada, the Netherlands, the UK and the US – with some politicians, political parties and the popular media energetically decrying foreign aid. Three main arguments are deployed to make the case against supporting the distant needy. Leading is the claim, mentioned above, that most foreign aid is wasted as the leaders and public servants of poor countries are invariably corrupt. While rich nations no longer routinely give aid directly to despots, and most aid agencies have sophisticated anti-corruption systems, the aid scandals that have emerged in Afghanistan and Iraq provide alarming evidence that corruption remains a major problem, especially in fragile states. Second comes the argument that foreign aid programmes are badly designed by rich-world bureaucrats and consultants who live off aid budgets. Aid projects do not help poor countries or poor people; they simply keep the 'aid industry' and 'beltway bandits' in jobs. Finally, there is the argument that the countries with the largest numbers of very poor people – India and China – are emerging powers that are 'better off than us'. Nowhere have these challenges led to the total cancellation of development cooperation, but they have helped constrain aid budgets in many OECD countries: one study found that US government spending on foreign aid values the lives of non-US citizens at 1/2,000th of the value of a US citizen.[8]

One might expect that the positive and negative arguments presented above would impact on public opinion in rich nations and, as most of these nations are democratic, on the very different levels of commitment to development described earlier. The evidence, from public opinion surveys in Europe and North America, is, however, paradoxical. While it indicates that the citizens of rich nations do not think about the distant poor very much, it also reveals that they think their governments should do something. For example, when 4,789 people in the UK were asked 'What is the most important issue facing Britain today?', only 10 (0.21%) mentioned global poverty. By contrast, in a different survey, when asked about global poverty, 25% declared themselves to be 'very concerned'.

But maybe this is paying too much attention to public opinion. If, as Colin Crouch argues,[9] many rich nations have moved into 'post-democratic' politics and the mass of the population have withdrawn from active political engagement, then we need to look at business and government elites to understand public policy. From this critical perspective the global poor have proved a useful adjunct to elite interests. Under the guise of 'reducing global poverty', business elites (and the political elites they resource) have been able to promote the economic liberalization of middle- and low-income countries so that the wealth of these elites has increased at an unprecedented rate. Alongside them official and civil society actors promoting global poverty reduction – bilateral aid agencies, the multilaterals (the UN and the World Bank), big-brand NGOs and even celebrities – have seen their budgets and/or profiles rise. By contrast, informed public understanding of and engagement with what governments are doing to support the distant needy appear to have receded – our leaders are permitted to do the right thing for the wrong reasons.

Who are the poor?

Whatever your motives, if you want to help the poor in faraway places, you have to be able to identify them. For several decades rich nations assumed that the rural populations of developing countries – countries that had not industrialized and had low GNIs per capita – were 'the poor'. Around 1990, however, rich nations began to adopt increasingly refined ways of identifying poor people.

The Oxford Dictionary defines poverty as the 'want of the necessities of life'. But there are fierce debates about what necessities are. While some of these debates are highly technical, most have a strong values dimension. Take, for example, the different ways of setting a poverty line: the minimum income that a person or family needs to meet their necessities. This can be done in absolute terms or relative terms. In poor countries absolute measures are used: the minimum income needed to meet the body's calorie needs and to provide basic shelter. Since 2015 the World Bank estimated this as around US$1.90 a day in poor countries (where purchasing power differences mean it buys more goods than in the rich world). By contrast, in the EU we measure poverty in relative terms. If someone has an income of less than 60% of their country's median income, then they are classed as poor. In Europe that means around US$20 to US$40 per person a day. In the US in 2015 it was US$32.25 a day for a single adult. With that a poor person can buy a varied diet, changes of clothing, have a television and a mobile phone – maybe even take their children to the zoo for their birthday. They are counted as *relatively poor* as they cannot do many of the things that the majority of their fellow citizens take for granted – going out to a restaurant, owning a laptop computer or having a foreign holiday. These contrasting measures are not just a technical choice; they mean that people officially classed as poor in a rich nation are much better-off in material terms than those classed as poor in a poor country.

For most in the rich world the mental image of the extreme poor is of women and children in emergency situations: after a cyclone or an earthquake, or running away from a violent conflict. Such humanitarian relief has always been an important part of rich-nation support for the distant needy, but it can obscure the evidence that most extremely poor people are trapped in grinding poverty. They are not simply the victims of a recent disaster or conflict. Instead, they (like their parents and grand-parents) make a living in a context that means they cannot meet their families' basic needs – even if they work 12 or 14 hours a day. For those lucky enough to just be able to meet their basic needs, conditions are very insecure – a sickness in the household, an accident at work, a downturn in the local labour market will see them slide into poverty again.

The ideas that you have about poverty are impor-tant. They shape 'who' you think is poor and 'what' should be done about it. If you see poverty simply as a lack of income, as many people do, then you are likely to see economic growth (and perhaps job creation) as the answer and look for market-based solutions. If you see poverty as multidimensional, then you are likely to also see a need for basic services (health, education, potable water, sanita-tion, etc.) and may well see a major role for public provision by the government. If you see poverty as caused by inequality or the abrogation of human rights, then you are likely to look for more radical action: the redistribution of economic assets and/or social and political power.

Allied to such contrasting value positions are deep-seated ideas about whether poverty is caused by individual or societal failings. These lead to the present-day contrast of 'strivers' and 'skivers' and the historical construct of the 'deserving poor' (widows, orphans, the elderly and the disabled) and the 'undeserving poor' (working-age people who cannot find jobs or earn enough to meet their family's needs).

The state of humanity: glass half full and glass half empty

Depending on the perspective you take you can argue that the last 25 years have been a period of unprecedented human progress or a great disappointment. The positive case focuses on the halving in the proportion of humanity living in extreme poverty since 1990, major improvements in health indicators (life expectancy and child survival) and other social indicators – Angus Deaton's 'great escape from poverty'.[10] The negative case argues that the number of people living in poverty (US$3.10-a-day income in 2011 prices) has barely changed since 1980, inequality has soared and our use of the global environment is unsustainable.

Why Worry About the Distant Poor?

There are many complex debates about whether things are getting better or not (see the Further Reading section), but three things are clear – at least to me. First, things have been 'getting better' for most of humanity, and at an increasing rate, over the last two centuries and especially over the last 25 years. Second, the rate of progress is too slow: there is an unacceptable amount of preventable human deprivation and suffering given our aggregate levels of wealth. Third, since the turn of the twenty-first century there has been an increasing perception of the precariousness of the quality of life – for both poor and non-poor people. The widespread mid-twentieth-century belief that 'my children's lives will be better than mine' is slipping away.

On the first point, economic and social conditions have been and are getting better for most of humanity. The UN data for 2015 estimate that the number of people living below the US\$1.25-a-day poverty line has fallen from 1.9 billion to 825 million since 1990: from 36% to 12% of the world population. Average per capita incomes continue to rise at a historically unprecedented rate (despite a growing human population). Life expectancy is up from 48 to 68 years since 1950; under-5 mortality has dropped from 90 deaths per 1,000 in 1990 to 43 in 2015; and many other social indicators have improved. At the regional and national level, patterns vary, but all regions of the world have made significant progress towards the UN MDGs. Only in a handful of countries (Iraq, Somalia, Syria and Zimbabwe) have such indicators got worse in the last 25 years.

There is no accepted or easy way of explaining exactly why things have been getting better. Many factors have helped: the creation and diffusion of relatively simple technical knowledge about health, hygiene, nutrition, organization and technologies (vaccines, feeding pregnant women, crop varieties, book-keeping, hand washing, cheap soap, piped water, etc.); trade and economic liberalization in many parts of the world; the end of the Cold War; China's return to the global economy; the commodity price super-cycle[11] in Africa; and many other factors. Leading thinkers on global development have increasingly moved away from a focus on 'getting the policies' right to 'getting the politics' right: the more complex terrain of making 'institutions', and especially the state, more effective.

Has progress been sufficient? We live in an affluent world: average gross global income per capita, a crude measure of affluence, has risen by almost 300%, from around US$2,100 in 1950 to more than US$7,800 in 2010.Yet around 3 billion people (out of 7 billion) experience limited access to the most basic of human needs: food, potable water and sanitation, basic health care and shelter. In our resource- and technology-rich world, around 20% to 40% of humanity (estimates vary) experiences basic needs deprivation on a daily basis. This has immediate effects, suffering and insecurity, and reduces (or terminates through preventable deaths) their future prospects for a good life and being productive.

And so to the third point, the precariousness of contemporary life – best presented as a strong personal feeling rather than an argument supported by empirical evidence. While almost all of the available evidence shows that most economic and social indicators are getting better, for many there does not seem to have been an accompanying improvement in perceptions of reduced vulnerability and enhanced future social security. This might be because of what philosophers call adaptive preferences: as things get better, maybe people take them for granted and expect even more. Alternatively, it might be because of changes in the media: rolling 24/7 news constantly telling us about all the bad things (and the trivial things) happening locally, nationally and globally; newspapers competing with each other by trying to have the most sensational stories – car accidents, murders and terror attacks – alongside celebrity marriage breakdowns and bad-hair days.

But perhaps a growing perception of insecurity is a rational response to contemporary circumstances. The continuing violence and ungovernability of Afghanistan, Iraq, Libya and Syria have shown that the might and resources of the world's most powerful country, supported by strong allies, cannot create peace and prosperity. Even more alarming, radical, political Islam appears to pit the West against ideologically/theologically powerful adversaries who are prepared to murder almost anyone anywhere. And the geopolitical context is changing so quickly: what is happening in Egypt after the Arab Spring, and in Turkey, which seemed to be a model Muslim-majority country? We live in a multi-polar world with Russia (or at least Putin and his allies) seeming hell-bent on behaving like a belligerent world power while its economy stagnates and its demography slides towards retirement. In sub-Saharan Africa the demographic problem is the reverse: with continuing high fertility and urbanization, how can its youth find jobs – by migrating to Europe? China is rattling its sabre in the South China Sea. Mexico, other Central American countries and, perhaps now, Peru seem to have organized crime deeply integrated into their state structures. International finance and banks do not appear to have changed their behaviours since the global crash of 2008, and cyber-crime against individuals, businesses and governments is spiralling. In a globalized economy, employment is increasingly insecure, and not just for poor people: in England and New England, middle-class parents wonder if their children will find secure jobs in a computerized/robotized world. And, after all these, there is still climate change to think about.

This uncertain context generates a number of responses. In most rich nations it has fostered the rise of right-wing political parties, ranging from UKIP in the UK to the Tea Party in the US, from the Front National in France to Fidesz in Hungary. These parties commonly present the distant needy ('economic migrants' and 'foreigners') as the cause of economic or social problems and counsel against cooperation with other countries and/or people with different identities. They deepen the political forces that argue against helping poor people in poor countries. Directly and indirectly, they often support vested interests that want to maintain 'business as usual': pretending climate change is not happening or is not a problem; minimizing immigration; and turning a blind eye to illicit behaviour by corporations.

And so a paradox: we live in a world in which the aggregate statistics suggest life is getting better, but so many people, including many of the better-off and middle classes, seem to be feeling more insecure.

Goodbye 'aid industry' . . . hello 'global partnership for development'

So, how might rich nations help poor nations and poor people prosper? The idea that this could be achieved simply by flows of foreign aid has waned, and, since around 2000, the idea of a global partnership for development (Goal 8 of the MDGs) has been identified as the way forward. But the first 15 years of attempting to forge such a partnership has produced only limited results. This is partly because the rich world – whether one envisions this as the G7/8, OECD, G20 or some other entity – finds it hard to agree on collective action. And it is partly because the economic and political elites in rich and emerging nations derive benefits from pursuing short-term self-interest: using foreign aid to achieve domestic political goals; making grand statements at the UN in New York but not resourcing them; promising trade policy reform but not changing policies; among others.

These obstacles could foster despair, but such pessimism would be unwise when life has been getting better for hundreds of millions of poor people in recent times. The challenge is to find ways of accelerating such progress while dealing with the rising problems of climate change and inequality. There are three main analytical elements to understanding this task. The first is improving foreign aid and the activities of international development agencies. This is the topic for chapter 2.

The second involves looking 'beyond aid' at the wider policies that are needed to support improved welfare for all. This entails understanding the dynamics of global poverty and prosperity, not simply in terms of foreign aid projects and the activities of multilateral development agencies, but in big picture terms: the evolution of global capitalism and the deeper historical processes of social and political change. In the twenty-first century – with a multi-polar world, the rise of BRICs (Brazil, Russia, India and China – and sometimes extended to South Africa), the commodity super-cycle, inequality rapidly rising and a revolution in connectivity – to understand 'how' rich nations can help poor countries and poor people, we need to look at the broader ways in which rich nations can help or hamper their prospects: trade, finance, migration, patterns of consumption, climate change, state-building and inequality.[12] These are the topics for chapters 3 and 4: analysing the wider economic and political processes of global development and identifying ways in which rich nations can really help the poor.

The recent shift from the MDGs to the UN Sustainable Development Goals creates a favourable environment for moving beyond the idea of international development as an aid 'project'. The key activity for rich nations is to move towards a genuine global, or near-global, partnership for economic and social progress: resolving the Doha impasse and agreeing a pro-poor trade round; agreeing on a climate justice settlement in which those who have contributed most to global climate change pay proportionately for mitigation and adaptation costs; restructuring the governance of key global institutions; staunching the haemorrhaging of finance out of developing countries through illicit financial transfers; and enhancing poor-nation access to development finance on reasonable terms.

In the conclusion I explore whether, and how, public support for reforming the policies and behaviour of rich nations towards the poor can be mobilized. This has been the missing ingredient of the 'global poverty eradication' efforts of the early twenty-first century. It has permitted many rich-world leaders to make public commitments to policy reforms at international summits, but then neglect such commitments in practice – as they do not experience sufficient domestic political pressure to have to keep their promises. Thinking about mobilizing public and elite support for the global poor means both thinking small (reducing your carbon footprint, joining a carefully selected NGO/ advocacy group, buying fair trade goods, talking to your neighbours) and thinking with grand ambition. How might an expanding and energized debate be created that will challenge national and international social norms so that around the world people who are 'doing OK' feel that poverty in an affluent world is both a moral outrage and an obstacle not only to their prospects of living well, but also to those of their children and grandchildren?

2

The Limits of Foreign Aid

In 2000 the UN's 189 member states unanimously declared: 'We will spare no effort to free our fellow men, women and children from the abject and dehumanizing conditions of extreme poverty, to which more than a billion of them are currently subjected. We are committed to ... freeing the entire human race from want.'[1] Since that declaration the world's rich nations (or at least the members of the OECD) have spent around US$ 2 trillion on eradicating poverty in poorer countries, but still almost one billion people live in extreme poverty and around three billion miss out on a basic human need. Has foreign aid failed, or have rich nations been too stingy, or is poverty eradication not primarily about foreign aid?

The Limits of Foreign Aid

Aid: quantity or quality?

Official development assistance is finance provided by a donor country to a recipient country (usually a low-income or a lower-middle-income country)[2] either as a grant or as a concessional loan (with interest rates below what financial markets would charge). For recipients, grants are much better than loans: the latter increase a poor country's debt burden, which can cause future problems. Aid volumes have to be carefully measured as deciding whether 'aid' is actually ODA is not always easy. Some aid is tied to imports from the donor country or contracts for natural resource extraction and it is difficult to assess whether it is genuinely concessional. Western critics of Chinese aid argue that it is commercial finance disguised as 'aid'. Westerners should be good at spotting such chicanery. Europe and the US declared vast amounts of export credits (to support their domestic corporations) as 'aid' in the mid- to late twentieth century.

While a substantial amount of ODA is *humanitarian*, to deal with disasters and emergencies, the bulk of foreign aid is provided for *national development*: to build roads and infrastructure, establish education and medical facilities, promote gender equality, make national governments more effective and help the private sector develop. Aid provided directly by one government to another is called *bilateral aid*. Aid transferred from a rich nation to a multilateral institution, such as the UN or World Bank, and then to poorer countries is called *multilateral aid*.

The origins of foreign aid date back to just after World War II with the Marshall Plan – US government support to rebuild war-torn Europe. This was probably the world's most successful aid programme ever. The rapid return of Europe to industrial growth and improved welfare meant that the Marshall Plan was judged a triumph (by the US and Europe). This fostered the idea that national development could be achieved by a massive infusion of ODA – a 'big push'. As decolonization gained momentum in the 1950s, rich countries established aid programmes in their former colonies. They talked of another Marshall Plan; however, the volume of their programmes was not at matching levels. The scale of ODA increased as the Cold War unfolded in the 1960s with the US and USSR trying to 'buy' allies. As remains the case today, although the declared aim of aid was to promote development in recipient countries, donor self-interest – commercial, geopolitical and diplomatic – strongly influenced the selection of recipients, the volumes of aid given and the uses to which it was put. Carol Lancaster has shown that while the dominant motive for donors to start aid programmes is usually self-interest, over time a 'moral vision' partly begins to shape such activities, but this differs greatly from country to country.[3]

After the end of the Cold War in 1990, foreign aid began steadily to decline, but the Jubilee Campaign for debt forgiveness, the MDGs and the Monterrey Finance for Development Summit in 2002 managed to stabilize and eventually raise aid levels. Between 2000 and 2005, net ODA increased from about US$80 billion to over US$120 billion and to US$135 billion in 2014 (Figure 2.1). Despite these recent increases it is evident that the net volume of ODA at 0.3% of rich nations' gross product is well below what they have persistently declared to be their target: 0.7%.

Historically, debates about foreign aid focused largely on aid volumes: whether the aggregate size of ODA was sufficient to achieve development goals and whether specific rich nations were making contributions proportional to their economic ability. While this remains a live debate, especially for aid flows to very poor nations with limited ability to generate public revenues, analysts have increasingly argued that for most recipient countries the key

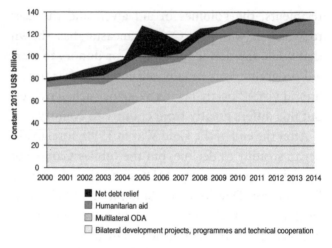

Figure 2.1. OECD/Development Assistance Committee (DAC) donors' net official development assistance (ODA), 2000–14

Source: OECD/DAC, '2014 ODA Tables and Charts', Paris, 8 April 2015 (www.oecd.org/dac/stats/documentupload/ODA%202014%20 Tables%20and%20Charts.pdf).

volume issue is not aid volume but overall access to finance for development. If this is the case, then the central issue for aid is whether it is effective, and particularly whether it can catalyse progressive economic, social and political change in recipient countries.

The Limits of Foreign Aid

Does aid work?

Fans of foreign aid can point to some amazing achievements. Aid-financed campaigns have eradicated smallpox globally and polio is close to eradication; insecticide-treated bed-nets have driven down infant mortality rates in sub-Saharan Africa; and millions of AIDS sufferers are alive and well today because of aid-financed access to retroviral medicines. The aid-financed 'Green Revolution' has doubled, tripled or quadrupled the traditional productivity of wheat and rice farmers in much of Asia. Across Africa and Asia the proportion of girls in schools has soared. Critics of aid point to a different set of examples. The aid provided to dictators like President Mobutu of the Democratic Republic of Congo (Zaïre) and President Banda of Malawi helped keep them in power while they impoverished their populations. Grants to Afghanistan since 2002 have been looted – much of the money seems to have been transferred directly from the Afghan Bank to secret bank accounts overseas within seconds of arrival. Halliburton has made excessive profits on solid waste removal contracts in Iraq. And the vast amounts of aid poured into Haiti do not appear to have done much for the welfare or economic prospects of its beleaguered people.

The Limits of Foreign Aid

The contesting sides of the aid effectiveness debate are easy to identify as some leading writers have adopted diametrically opposed views (though, as we shall see, it may be the more nuanced analysts with less polarized positions who offer the most useful practical advice). At one extreme are writers who argue that aid is largely effective. These are led by Jeffrey Sachs, senior adviser to UN secretary-generals Kofi Annan and Ban Ki-moon, with his argument that the MDGs were fully achievable by 2015. All that was needed was more ODA. According to Sachs, the knowledge, technology and organizational capacity to reach the MDGs existed: if donors had just contributed more aid ($121 billion extra in 2006 rising to $189 billion in 2015), the targets could have been achieved in all regions of the world.

At the opposite end of the spectrum, and sometimes reducing Sachs to tears in public debates, is Bill Easterly with his books *The Tyranny of Experts* and *The White Man's Burden*. While Easterly does not argue that all foreign aid has failed, the data he presents make it feel that way. He chides Sachs' over-optimism and points the finger at proponents of aid such as former UK Prime Minister Gordon Brown:

> Gordon Brown was silent about the other tragedy of the world's poor ... the tragedy in which the West spent $2.3 trillion on foreign aid over the last five decades and still had not managed to get twelve-cent medicines to children to prevent half of all malaria deaths ... to get three dollars to each new mother to prevent five million child deaths ... that so much well-meaning compassion did not bring these results for needy people.[4]

For Easterly, what is needed is less aid – and much more effectiveness.

It is Dambisa Moyo who holds the most extreme anti-aid position. In *Dead Aid* she argues that '[a]id remains at the heart of the development agenda despite ... very compelling reasons to show that it perpetuates the cycle of poverty and derails sustainable economic growth.'[5] Her withering attack claims that ODA corrupts African governments and encourages African elites and middle classes to pocket aid rather than run governments or businesses. From this perspective aid has not merely been ineffective, it has been destructive. Foreign aid should be stopped immediately, so that private finance and markets can work their magic.

These polar positions help us to identify the arguments for and against aid, but they say relatively little about the detail of using aid more effectively. Sachs' exaggeration of the state of knowledge – in effect his claim that science now provides a cure for poverty and all that is needed is more money – provides a damagingly inaccurate assessment of levels of understanding. Easterly's erudite cynicism does not provide practical advice that outweighs its damaging pessimism. And although it is wonderful to have an African woman deliberating on these issues (rather than the usual ageing white males – myself included), Moyo's blanket dismissal of aid neglects the evidence that some aid, albeit not enough, is improving the prospects of Africa's poor: paying for them to attend school, be vaccinated, survive AIDS, avoid malaria and escape Ebola infection.

To understand the heated debates surrounding aid effectiveness it is necessary to look closely at the arguments behind the 'aid works' and 'aid fails' positions. These are based on (i) case studies of aid project and programme performance, (ii) theoretical positions and (iii) econometric assessments of whether countries that have received more aid have experienced faster economic growth or greater poverty reduction. The first form of evidence depends on the selection of cases that are made: it can be rigged by selecting mainly favourable examples (a criticism levelled at Sachs) or mainly unfavourable examples (a criticism levelled at Moyo). The second

set of arguments revolves around contrasting theoretical propositions. The aid optimists continue
to theorize that a 'big push', a massive infusion
of ODA, will shock poor countries into economic
growth and human development. The aid pessimists
hypothesize that aid crowds out private sector
investment, threatens macroeconomic stability and
causes 'Dutch disease'.[6] The predictive capacity of
these theories depends on the degree to which the
assumptions that underpin them (perfect governments or perfect markets) match, or do not match,
real-world situations.

The results of the econometric exercises depend
on the models that are specified, the underlying assumptions and the availability and quality
of data.[7] The technical sophistication of attempts
by exceptionally clever people to prove that 'aid
works', or to prove that 'aid fails', should not
distract us from asking whether such exercises are
futile. The Nobel Prize-winning economist Angus
Deaton warns that 'researchers have expended an
enormous amount of ingenuity – and even more
foolishness – on trying to disentangle the effects
of aid on growth'.[8] In practice, we know that aid
does work (in some forms, in some places, at some
times) and also that aid fails (in some forms, in
some places, at some times). Knowing whether the

average result of historical interventions is positive or negative is of limited relevance for contemporary policy. The knowledge that is required is about the selection of forms of aid that will work in specific countries at specific times and how to avoid ineffective or damaging aid programming.

Roger Riddell's *Does Foreign Aid Really Work?* stands out as a painstaking analysis of what is known about aid policy and outcomes.[9] The good practices include untying aid from donor country products and services; using aid to put cash directly into the hands of poor people; making aid more predictable; implementing agreed reforms on donor coordination (such as the Paris Declaration) rather than donors having a multitude of small and often competing projects; reducing policy conditionality; and letting recipients determine their own economic policy.

On the other side of the aid relationship, poor countries, the increasing recognition that national development is very much determined by historically evolving processes of state formation (not policies or projects) makes the results of aid programming inherently unpredictable. As Nancy Birdsall and her colleagues argue, perhaps the greatest problem of a focus on aid effectiveness is that 'countries most in need of aid are often those least able to use it well'.[10]

In countries with the deepest poverty and the greatest need for aid the commitment and the capacity of governments and leaders to use aid effectively is often at its lowest. In such contexts – Afghanistan, the Democratic Republic of Congo, Haiti, Somalia and 50 to 60 others – providing ODA and using it effectively may be only a small part of a strategy for tackling extreme poverty.

New kids on the block: China, the BRICs . . . Bill & Melinda

Annoyingly, at a time when our knowledge and understanding of the foreign aid provided by rich nations are greatly improving, the entire game of giving aid has transformed. The rise of China and, to a lesser degree, the other BRICs, alongside the rise of mega-wealthy trusts such as the Bill & Melinda Gates Foundation, has transformed the context for aid giving. In the past poor countries had to agree to IMF and World Bank policies and conditionalities before donors (the members of the OECD and multilaterals) would give them ODA. The aid that countries received from these 'traditional donors' had to fit in with rich-country aid policies: promoting women in development in the 1980s, promoting good governance in the 1990s, and so on. With the arrival of China as an aid donor, things have changed. Poor countries now have a choice. They can take their aid from OECD countries; or they can take their aid from 'non-traditional donors' such as China (and to a lesser degree India or Brazil). If they play their cards carefully, they can take aid from both sources at the same time. While traditional donors will try to determine aid use according to their ODA policies and set conditions, the Chinese approach has been to fund whatever developing country governments, and especially their leaders, identify as priorities.

China's aid programme has expanded massively since 2000. However, it is difficult to determine how much of its foreign aid and government-sponsored investment activity (FAGIA) would actually meet OECD/DAC definitions of ODA. Many FAGIA loans have only a small subsidy element. Indeed, the difficulties of determining what proportion of Chinese development finance could be classed as ODA make the analysis of global aid volumes increasingly imprecise. Nevertheless, with a pledged volume of US$189 billion in 2011, even if figures are exaggerated this represents a vast amount of investment.[11] Much of this aid/FAGIA is provided bilaterally to poor-country governments with a particular concentration on infrastructural projects (roads, bridges, railways and irrigation canals), sometimes with repayments tied to natural resource extraction by Chinese companies. Analyses of the 'aid effectiveness' of such aid/FAGIA are in their infancy, with commentators tending to determine their findings by making negative or positive assumptions about the benefits of infrastructure and the costs of resource extraction and debt servicing. Some studies believe that massive infrastructural investment in productivity-enhancing infrastructure will stimulate growth (especially in Africa). Alongside this, strengthening the position of poor-country governments to negotiate with the IMF/ World Bank, it is argued, will allow poor countries to pursue more heterodox macroeconomic policies for jobs and growth. Other analysts reach quite different conclusions. They find that Chinese FAGIA and associated deals on future access to minerals and hydrocarbons will create a new wave of highly indebted poor countries. In addition, they argue that China's support for 'bad' regimes (Robert Mugabe in Zimbabwe, Omar al-Bashir in Sudan and José Eduardo dos Santos in Angola) fosters bad governance.

But China is not just providing finance bilaterally. It is also playing an increasing role in multilateral finance for development. Some of this finance is programmed for the Asian Development Bank (ADB), but China has been unhappy with Japanese control of this institution and has taken the lead in setting up the Asian Infrastructure Investment Bank (AIIB), which will directly compete with the ADB. China is also playing a leading role in the BRICS (the BRICs and South Africa), which have agreed to set up competitor institutions to the IMF and World Bank (see chapter 3 under 'Finance').

A significant proportion of aid for poverty reduction is channelled through NGOs alongside the charitable donations that those organizations collect. Indeed, the public in rich nations are much more aware of the big-brand NGOs – Oxfam, CARE, Save the Children, World Vision and others – than they are of their official, bilateral aid agencies. The big-brand NGOs have strong reputations, although often there is only limited empirical evidence about their performance. Alongside these NGOs the last decade has witnessed the rise of philanthro-capitalists tackling global poverty. However, with the exception of the Gates Foundation, most of the 'big' philanthropists are relatively small in terms of bilateral and multilateral aid volumes. Nevertheless, the influence of philanthropists (and related corporate social responsibility initiatives) may be greater than the additional funds they contribute to poverty reduction. In particular their zealous promotion of microfinance – despite the evidence that it has a relatively minor impact on poverty levels – reveals the way that philanthropy can shape public understanding. No wonder they have been accused of using their charities to promote neo-liberal capitalism, and the associated rising inequality, as good for the poor.

The Gates Foundation (financed by Bill Gates and Warren Buffett) is a significant source of additional finance in its own right. It has already given away grants exceeding US$30 billion between 2000 and 2015. While evaluations of the Foundation provide evidence of its beneficial short-term impacts on poor people, its contribution to development is challenged in two main ways. The first is that its focus on 'vertical delivery programmes' for vaccinations has blocked the evolution of national health care systems which can tackle the range of major health problems poor people face and not just ones where there is an easy technical fix. The second is that it is anti-democratic. This was spelled out to me in Uganda in 2012. One of my students asked the Minister of Health: 'What will be the future health care priorities in Uganda?' The Minister replied: 'Don't ask me, ask Bill Gates. He will decide what he wants to fund, the aid donors will follow him and that will become Uganda's priority.'

It's the politics, stupid

An increasingly influential literature argues that the role of aid agencies and external actors in development has been greatly exaggerated. Birdsall and her colleagues write that 'development is something largely determined by poor countries themselves, and that outsiders can play only a limited role . . . financial aid . . . [has] only a limited ability to trigger growth, especially in the poorest countries'.[12] Deep-seated institutional or governance problems, not lack of resources, are viewed as the main issues.

Since the end of the Cold War, aid and development agencies have distinguished between operations in 'stable' and 'fragile' countries, in the belief that the natural state of any developing country is peace, political stability and a functioning government. Countries which are not in this condition need special treatment until they stabilize. If only the world was so simple. In *Why Nations Fail*, Daron Acemoglu and James Robinson point out the lunacy of such a position:[13] only around 35 to 40 of the world's 200-plus countries have actually achieved political stability, the rule of law and effective governance. The vast majority of countries are still engaged in the early stages of state formation or are struggling towards 'good enough governance' (good enough to permit improvements in economic growth and basic welfare). With the wisdom of hindsight we know that donor efforts to impose 'good governance' on poor countries in the 1990s – parliaments, multi-party elections, anti-corruption agencies, decentralization and privatization of public corporations – caused as much harm as good (look at what happened in Russia).

From this standpoint the priority tasks for well-meaning foreigners and aid agencies are to (i) meet humanitarian needs so that people can survive, and (ii) reduce the prospects of corrupt national elites pillaging the economy and weakening public institutions (such as parliament, the judiciary, police and civil service). In such analyses 'context is king' – to contribute to progress, any intervention needs to be based on a deep understanding of the political economy, social structures and leaders of a country and its sub-regions. This is an uncomfortable message for aid agencies, who have long presented aid as a technical solution to well-defined problems. It suggests that their attempts to assist poor countries will not merely need a political analysis but will need to directly engage in political change in sovereign states (what can be called political interference). Compounding this, publicly admitting the unpredictability of trying to assist poor countries (or poor people in poor countries) is likely to frighten domestic taxpayers. What point would there be in giving aid to another country if you were not sure of beneficial outcomes? And anyway, 'charity begins at home'.

From aid projects to the big picture

In his book *The Bottom Billion* Paul Collier concludes that '[a]id does have serious problems, and more especially serious limitations . . . but it is part of the solution rather than part of the problem. The challenge is to complement it with other actions.'[14] So, how might we improve aid effectiveness, and what are the 'other actions'?

Improving the contribution of aid to poverty reduction is a complex task, but some of the steps are very clear. First, untie aid (this means not just buying goods and services from the donor country). This reduces the costs of delivering aid-financed goods and services and increases the prospects for using goods and services from poorer countries (from the recipient country or from neighbouring developing countries). Why ship expensive US grain across the Atlantic when African countries can supply emergency food aid at lower costs and more quickly? Second, use aid to put cash directly into the hands of poor and very poor people. Cash transfers are proving remarkably effective at reducing poverty in the short term and promoting human development in the medium and longer term. Third, prioritize aid to create pro-poor public goods. This is especially important for the major health problems of poor people, as such diseases are a low priority for rich-world pharmaceutical and health corporations, and for tropical agricultural research, which is under-funded. Fourth, improve the processes of aid delivery: make aid volumes more predictable so that their use can be planned; improve donor coordination by implementing agreed reforms; reduce policy conditionality and permit recipient governments to chart national economic policy. None of these reforms require rocket science. There is a clear body of evidence showing the benefits that would derive from each of them and all are relatively straight-forward to implement – if they have political support.

And if one moves 'beyond aid' to the big picture, what are the complementary policy changes that rich nations could pursue? These are much more challenging to advance as they confront the vested interests of economically and politically powerful groups in rich nations. They are discussed in later chapters, but we shall list them here:

- *Reform international trade policies* so that poor countries and poor people can gain a greater share of the benefits derived from trade.
- *Recognize international migration* as an element of trade policy and a highly effective means of reducing poverty.
- *Take action against climate change* (mitigation and supporting adaptation) and take responsibility for the historical role of rich nations in creating global warming.
- *Reform global finance* to stop the siphoning off of income and assets from poor countries to rich countries (by corporations and national elites).
- *Limit the arms trade to fragile countries* and regions and carefully consider support for *military action* (budgets, technology and even 'feet on the ground') in specific cases, such as the successful Operation Palliser in Sierra Leone.

This brief list is an *aide-mémoire*. Let's look in more detail at what tackling the big picture would look like.

3

What Can Be Done?

If foreign aid is not the main way for rich nations to help the poor, then what policies would make a big difference? How could poor countries be incorporated into contemporary capitalism so that economic growth would be promoted equitably and sustainably? Let's start with growth.

The elusive quest for growth[1]

Rich nations, and the multilateral development agencies they control, have long prescribed economic growth as the cure for poverty. But at the same time, according to Ha-Joon Chang, they have often been 'bad Samaritans' and undermined economic growth prospects in developing countries.[2] This has to stop: rich nations must become good Samaritans.

What Can Be Done?

Contemporary policy debates concerning how to achieve economic growth that is job-creating and welfare-promoting have evolved out of theorizing about growth in Western Europe, North America and East Asia. Central to these debates are heated arguments about the comparative roles of the state and the market. Ideologues of the Left see the state as delivering development: only the state can provide the public goods (law and order, human capital, infrastructure) that underpin growth and stop the private sector from exploiting workers and the poor. On the Right, the state is seen as the main obstacle to development: just leave things to the market, growth will ensue and poverty will reduce as the benefits of economic growth 'trickle down'. In the 1950s and 1960s most developing countries stayed away from these extreme positions, opting for the middle ground of a state-guided, mixed-economy strategy – recommended by the UN and the World Bank with the support of the US and its allies. This strategy pursued growth through import-substituting industrialization, protecting infant industries, and was often centred on a Five-Year National Plan. The radical alternative strategy – state-controlled, 'communist' development based on delinking from the capitalist world economy and totalitarian central planning – was pursued by only a few countries: Burma, Cambodia, China, Cuba, North Korea and North Vietnam. With the exception of Cuba, where the status of health and education rapidly improved, these autarkic strategies proved disastrous for growth and were associated with repression and even holocausts (Cambodia and China).

Everything changed with the global ascendancy of neo-liberal thinking in the late 1970s and the debt crisis of the 1980s. In most aid-recipient countries IMF- and World Bank-designed 'structural adjustment programmes' were adopted and/or imposed. These focused on rolling back the state and giving the private sector responsibility for virtually all economic development activity and increasing amounts of social policy. The Washington Consensus mantra of 'privatization, liberalization and deregulation' sought to create unfettered markets delivering growth and welfare. The theoretically perfect markets underpinning these models did not match reality, however. In many countries growth remained low and/or slowed down when the structural adjustment medicine was taken. Sometimes, poverty deepened, especially for low-income urban households and women. With the introduction of 'user fees', access to basic health and primary education services was catastrophically reduced for many poor people. Over the 1990s concerns about the lack of growth and adverse consequences of structural adjustment led to the moderation of these policies. Active debate about economic strategy returned. This contrasted the IMF/World Bank liberalization and growth strategy with the UN's human development strategy based on major roles for the state, market and civil society and greater spending on health and education.

These debates are now very nuanced, with leading researchers and development agencies arguing about how growth can be made pro-poor (through market or state action?), the relative prioritization of human development policies (which contribute most to well-being and which contribute most to future economic growth?) and the best forms of service delivery (public or private or public–private partnerships?). This does not mean that everyone is 'in the centre', as some strategies, and the hybrid policies within them, are closer to a Washington Consensus position, while others are much closer to a state-led mixed-economy position. The World Bank Research Department and successive *World Development Reports* have moved significantly closer to the UN position since the late 1990s, recognizing the central role of the state in development and the problems that rising inequality creates for tackling poverty. Even researchers at the IMF are now worried that income inequality is bad for growth.

However, this gradual shift of position in the World Bank and IMF's research findings has not been accompanied by an equivalent shift in their policy guidance. Within and between these two agencies there have been heated contestations about which policies are best. Joseph Stiglitz, a Nobel Prize-winning economist, was forced to resign from the Bank for highlighting evidence revealing that orthodox IMF stabilization programmes stalled economic growth. An authoritative, independent evaluation of the Bank's research on growth found that 'much of this line of research appears to have such deep flaws that at present, the results cannot be regarded as remotely reliable'.[3] The Bank's Research Department had used relatively untested research that supported a pro-liberalization stance to 'proselytize on behalf of Bank policy, often without taking a balanced view of the evidence, and without expressing appropriate skepticism. Internal research that was favorable to Bank positions was given great prominence, and unfavorable research ignored.'

The free market orientation of World Bank and IMF positions has softened in recent years and the

Bank's public statements have moved closer to UN-type positions with its increased sectoral eclecticism (countries need to pursue growth, human development and better governance). But major debates remain about whether the Bank, like the IMF, still prioritizes macroeconomic stability and economic growth to such a degree that expenditures on education, health and social protection are constrained, increasing present-day suffering and reducing the potential for people to contribute to future economic growth and social progress. It is clear that the IMF's neo-liberal culture remains very much intact despite the increasingly 'heterodox' findings of its researchers. This is vividly illustrated by evidence that IMF-imposed health expenditure controls on West African countries fuelled the Ebola crisis of 2014–15.[4]

Regardless of IMF and World Bank prescriptions, poor countries are now trying to shift to more heterodox strategies. This is partly because of the considerable evidence that macroeconomic strategies guided by well-planned state intervention create poverty-reducing growth. But, even more significantly, it is because the ability of the IMF and the World Bank to impose policies reduces when alternative sources of finance are available. These have come from the commodity price boom of

2002–13 and loans and investment from China and the BRICS coming on stream.

In recent years, as many countries in the developing world (including several in sub-Saharan Africa) have witnessed steady economic growth, there has been an interest among Southern governments and international agencies in creating a pattern of growth that can be sustained over time – 'structural transformation'. Without structural transformation – the rapid movement of workers from low-productivity traditional sectors to high-productivity modern sectors – economic growth has proved to be prone to 'boom and bust'. Critics of Washington Consensus policies have demonstrated that structural transformation occurs without prioritizing economic liberalization. The East Asian Tigers achieved structural transformation by first pursuing carefully implemented trade and industrial policies, without improving economic policy fundamentals or becoming democratic. These critics – Ha-Joon Chang, Ricardo Hausmann, Lant Pritchett, Dani Rodrik, Joseph Stiglitz, and others – are increasingly seen as offering authoritative analyses based on the understanding of real-world contexts (messy and varying) rather than sophisticated, assumption-based models of what is best for the hypothetical 'average poor country'.

What Can Be Done?

The debate on the role of the state versus the market has taken a new turn. There has been a convergence in thinking that in low-income countries, structural transformation is not possible if it is left to the market – both state and market are essential for sustained growth. The state has an important role to play in technological upgrading of economic activity and in providing infrastructure (roads and ports) and schooling that modern sectors need to expand. At the same time, structural transformation is not possible without a dynamic capitalist sector and the growth of modern private firms with entrepreneurial and management abilities and skilled workers to compete in a globalized economy.

Finance: does telling Mali to behave like Denmark work?

Common sense has at last arrived in discussions about finance for development. After decades of international development agencies highlighting the role of foreign aid and lauding foreign direct investment (FDI), there is a realization that domestic resource mobilization is central to national development. The UN's Open Working Group on

What Can Be Done?

Sustainable Development Goals and the Secretary-General's High-Level Panel recognize the primacy of 'strengthen[ing] domestic resource mobilization ... [to] improve domestic capacity for tax and other revenue collection'. No longer neglected, the most important source of finance for development, domestic resources, is now at the centre of the agenda. And it needs to be. Not only because it already provides the bulk of resources in most low- and middle-income countries, but also because it ensures national ownership of development strategies and is more predictable than aid and FDI.

So, the key finance question for development is: 'How can more domestic resources be mobilized?' The standard answer is: 'Raise the tax effort (the percent of GDP being collected as revenue) by following international best practice.' But telling Mali to behave like Denmark rarely works. If tax reform was so easy, then 35 years of EU membership would surely have achieved more in Greece. Tax is 'sticky', and major reforms often produce only small changes as they are watered down by key interest groups. In many poor countries the aid donor recommended introduction of VAT and the establishment of Semi-Autonomous Revenue Agencies (SARAs) has produced only modest increases in tax effort. Low tax effort may be less about tax systems and more about the economic structure of poor countries. You cannot expect a country whose population largely consists of poor people in dispersed rural communities to be taxed at the 35% to 45% levels now achieved in the OECD. This takes decades, entailing incremental progressive changes in state capacity and social norms alongside a shift towards a more formal economy. But progress is possible. Tanzania, for example, raised its share of revenues to GDP from 9.6% in 2001/2 to 14.6% in 2009/10.

Taxation and royalties from natural resource extraction – minerals, metals, oil and gas – are a special concern. There is substantial evidence of a 'resource curse', or, more accurately a 'political resource curse', in poorer countries. Accountability and democratic processes seem to be undermined in developing countries reliant on natural resource extraction, levels of corruption are high and the other productive sectors (agriculture and manufacturing) are neglected in public policy and by business elites. Average GNI per capita soars while jobless growth, weak social policy and a breakdown in state–citizen relationships deliver deepening poverty. Nigeria is the classic example of the resource curse, but there are many others. Since the early 1970s when oil was 'found', the country has earned hundreds of billions of dollars from oil exports but 46%

of its population still live on less than US$1.25 a day. While the Nigerian elite own private jets and homes in Houston, London and Geneva, half of their compatriots live without water, sanitation or electricity.

International support to use natural resource wealth more inclusively has often prescribed 'best practice'. That usually means trying to set up a sovereign wealth fund modelled on Norway or Chile, but this has produced few results. When oil and gas were found in Ghana recently, groups of officials visited Norway to learn about its management of oil revenues. And yet in 2014 the government of Ghana had to seek an emergency loan from the IMF – it had borrowed so much money on the basis of its future oil wealth that it could not meet the repayment schedule. Since then the price of oil has halved. Ask a Ghanaian if oil is a blessing or a curse, and I think you can guess the answer.

Natural resource extraction is commonly associated with illicit or illegal transfers of money (electronically or in suitcases filled with US$100 bills) and commodities by national elites and MNCs. Such illicit flows are common in many other sectors. The UN Economic Commission for Africa estimates that the continent loses 'more than US$50 billion' every year from illicit financial flows. According to Global Financial Integrity (GFI), large numbers of international companies operating in developing countries use tax havens to bleed countries' royalties and revenues. Despite vast turnovers and decades of operation they continuously declare small profits, or break-even trading, through transfer-mispricing. It works like this. A multinational food company sets up a factory in Ghana and soon makes profits of US$10 million a year. However, because it makes large payments to a sister company in Switzerland for use of the company brand, and to an affiliate in Jersey for 'management services', its profits in Ghana are reported as zero. By shifting its profits out of Ghana, where the corporation tax rate is 25%, into a tax haven where it can be 0%, the company reduces its overall tax bill to almost zero, and Ghana loses out on US$2.5 million tax revenue. According to GFI, for every US$1 of ODA and FDI that developing countries receive there is an illicit outflow of US$10. These figures are estimates, but even if they are overestimates, the losses of revenue to poorer countries are enormous.

A vast and well-paid network of lawyers, accountants and financiers based in offshore tax havens supports MNCs in profit-shifting and wealthy people in hiding their ownership of companies. As the UK government found out, when revelations about tax avoidance by Vodafone, Starbucks and

Google hit the headlines, using tax havens to shift profits and avoid tax bills has become hardwired into the business model of many large multinationals. Fortunately for poorer countries, this has incensed several rich nations, and the G20, and subsequently the G8 and the OECD (who set international tax rules), have begun to take seriously tax avoidance by MNCs. But do not underestimate the resistance to change. These corporations are economically and politically very powerful.

There are other big changes afoot in finance for development. In 2014 the leaders of the BRICS announced the creation of the New Development Bank (NDB), with US$50 billion in capital to finance infrastructure and sustainable development projects in developing countries, and the Contingent Reserve Arrangement (CRA), to provide emergency finance to countries facing financial crisis. The NDB and the CRA, respectively, will be taking on roles that have usually been undertaken by the World Bank and the IMF. If the BRICS evolve the collaborative capacity to manage these institutions effectively, and expand their capital base, then the options for finance for development and 'crisis' loans for developing countries will widen – and the need to agree to IMF/World Bank loan conditionalities will reduce.

What Can Be Done?

The key priority in contemporary finance for development negotiations is to focus on the big issues: mobilizing domestic finance; stamping out illicit and illegal financial flows from poorer countries to tax havens; enhancing private flows; utilizing remittances more effectively; making ODA more predictable; reforming the governance of the World Bank and the IMF; and helping an expanded set of plurilateral institutions evolve.

Trade policy: from free trade to fair trade

While trade policy in poor countries does not set the rich world's media on fire, it has become a part of everyday life for the citizens of Europe and North America. Try buying a cup of coffee in London or Ottawa which is not certified 'fair trade'. Trade in food and intellectual property rights, especially medicines, are particular concerns for poor nations. However, while outrage about rich countries dictating trade policies to poor countries closed Seattle down with violent street protests in 1999, this has now faded away. To get fair trade back on the agenda the inelegant idea of 'unreciprocated' trade bargains (deals where rich nations permit poor countries improved access to their markets without

68

having to make equivalent concessions) needs to gain traction.

The great trade debates of history and today are between 'free trade' and protectionist policies. In the nineteenth century these debates, and sometimes protests, were part of day-to-day life in Manchester (my academic base). On one side was the Anti-Corn Law League (intellectuals supported by factory owners and factory workers) promoting 'free trade' in agriculture so that urban food prices could be lowered by grain imports from Canada – making food cheaper for workers and reducing wage costs for industrialists. On the other side were the politically powerful landed gentry opposing the repeal of the 'Corn Laws' that placed high tariffs on wheat imports. Eventually free trade (in grain) won the day and Manchester prospered as the world's first industrial city, although perhaps this should be qualified, for this was 'free trade' as defined by powerful imperial interests which stopped colonies from manufacturing cotton goods.

Fast forward to the 1980s and 1990s, when neo-liberal thinking fostered a wave of full-blooded trade liberalization around the world. This unleashed a period of globalization that has seen economic growth rates soar in Asia (especially China and India) but which has left many countries (and one to three billion people) in poverty. In the early twenty-first century the trade debates have returned. Increasingly, debate within both the powerful World Trade Organization (WTO) and academic circles centres on the need for 'policy space' or 'development space' for developing countries in their trade relations.

For critics of the free trade orthodoxy and the WTO, such as Robert Wade, 'the "development space" for diversification and upgrading policies in developing countries is being shrunk'.[5] Wade and like-minded scholars argue that developing countries need to be able to energetically use targeted trade protection to shelter their infant industries while they build themselves up into a position in which they are able to compete in global markets. In support of this they point to the policies of those countries that have successfully industrialized. History, they tell us, shows that trade protection has to be a component of the drive for prosperity. Proponents of the 'policy space' view argue that developing countries need to be able to repeat these successful policies, and that the WTO therefore needs to permit them to raise tariffs if necessary.

Those more in favour of free trade – the rich nations and MNCs – take an opposite position. They argue that the blocking of trade protectionism by WTO agreements is one of the key benefits of WTO membership for developing countries: it prevents governments from giving in to pressure from domestic interests for protection of inefficient industries. Rich nations and Western MNCs also have the advantage that their powerful economic position allows them to define the forms that free trade policy should take: open markets for rich-world products and protected markets for products where poor countries have a comparative advantage.

The creation of the WTO in 1995 was seen as a major advance as it extended multilateral trade regulation far beyond the area of industrial goods that its predecessor, the General Agreement on Tariffs and Trade (GATT), had focused on. Notably, the WTO regulates agricultural trade, although it soon became clear that the Agreement on Agriculture was severely flawed. Those flaws have meant that agriculture continues to be the most contentious part of trade negotiations, creating difficulties for both developed and developing countries. In the present round of negotiations – the interminable Doha Round, which started in 2001 – the industrialized countries have been unwilling to offer cuts to the subsidies that they pay to their farmers, despite the damage these subsidies do to farmers in developing

71

countries. A particular bone of contention has been the subsidies paid to US cotton farmers, which depress world cotton prices by 26%, reducing the income of cotton farmers elsewhere. The issue has been championed by the 'Cotton Four' – Burkina Faso, Benin, Chad and Mali – some of the poorest countries in the world.

Liberalization of agriculture has also been problematic for developing countries that have large numbers of relatively inefficient, small-scale farmers. Such countries, led by India, are wary of opening up their markets to cheap agricultural imports, fearful that this will devastate the livelihoods of peasant farmers and lead to governments being voted out of office. To protect food and livelihood security, developing countries have argued that, in any Doha Round deal, they must be allowed a certain number of 'special products' that can still be protected. A 'special safeguard mechanism' will be put in place, but the exact details of this mechanism have proven almost impossible to negotiate, as the farmer-agribusiness lobbies in many rich countries, especially the US and France, are very powerful political constituencies that national governments (and Presidents) will not confront. Hope that the rich nations, emerging powers and developing countries might reach a deal was ignited at the

WTO's Bali Summit in December 2013, but this unravelled over the following year.[6]

The other especially contentious area between the rich world and poorer countries is intellectual property. The Agreement on Trade-Related Intellectual Property Rights (TRIPs), signed in 1994, made countries apply minimum standards of copyright and intellectual property protection. TRIPs subsequently received a great deal of criticism for raising the costs of AIDS drugs to poor countries. They had previously been importing generic drugs that are up to 90% cheaper than branded drugs. As a result, many Africans (probably hundreds of thousands and perhaps millions) who could have survived AIDS died prematurely. Pressure from NGOs, especially in South Africa, developing countries and the gay community (in the US and Europe) eventually led to an agreement in 2003 making it easier for poor countries to import generic drugs. However, this decision requires an onerous and bureaucratic procedure to be completed, slowing down access to critical drugs. Meanwhile, the original justification for the inclusion of TRIPs in the Uruguay Round agreement – that it would increase research-and-development spending by rich-world pharmaceutical companies on diseases prevalent in poor countries – has been found not to have been borne out. This is across the board for tropical diseases but is most clearly evidenced by the lack of research on Ebola.

It gets worse. TRIPs is not the most restrictive rich-nation practice limiting poor-country access to intellectual property rights. With WTO negotiations making little headway, many rich nations have been pursuing bilateral (between two countries) and plurilateral (involving a group of countries) free trade agreements with developing countries. The EU and US lead on this. They present these as win-win agreements; however, the political and technical strength of the bargaining position of the US and EU, compared to low-income governments, has led many commentators to see this shift as undermining the multilateral, non-discriminatory system embodied in the WTO, leading to a 'spaghetti bowl' of competitive, preferential agreements.[7]

One popular response to the complex debates about the role of international trade in promoting economic growth and poverty reduction has been the evolution of a campaign for fair trade.[8] This directly seeks to ensure that poor people receive a higher price for crops they grow – especially coffee, tea and cocoa. Depending on your perspective, this can be seen as a form of charity, voluntarily agreeing to pay a little more, or as a means of overcoming market imperfections: small farmers have a weak negotiating position with traders and MNCs, and paying a fair price helps to correct this information and power asymmetry. Campaigners for fair trade point to two beneficial results of their efforts. First, the incomes of some poor people are increased, with knock-on effects to the vibrancy of local economies. Second, fair trade provides a platform for raising the awareness of rich-world consumers about poverty, and particularly about 'working poverty' in poor countries. It deepens the appreciation of the invisible global connections through which rich and poor people interact.

These efforts are often treated condescendingly by orthodox economists, who see such campaigners as naïve do-gooders. They have two main arguments. First, fair trade discourages economic diversification. Producers get higher prices as long as they continue growing the crops that have locked them into poverty. Second, fair trade raises levels of production and this reduces the prices for all the other producers. However, it is erroneous to claim, dismissively, as influential commentators such as Martin Wolf of the *Financial Times* do, that 'the fair-trade movement probably makes virtually no difference'.[9] This is not so much because of the direct impact of fair trade; it is because of the indirect impact of the movement. Anti-fair trade economists do not recognize the contribution that fair trade ideas make to changing social norms in the rich world. The sorts of 'unreciprocated' trade bargains espoused by fair trade critic Paul Collier, to shift the WTO towards a genuine development round, are more likely to be supported by countries in which there is a domestic political constituency promoting less nationalistic trade relations with poor countries. The fair trade campaign is the main way in which voters and future voters (school-children) understand how unjust the present world trade system is.

Migration: 'the most powerful tool for reducing global poverty'

In marked contrast to international trade, international migration is headline news and a contentious public issue in rich nations. President Obama's 2014 decision to grant millions of illegal migrants US citizenship infuriated tens of millions in the US. They would rather he deported more people and speeded up building the Border Barrier between the US and Mexico. During 2015 more than one million migrants, many of them refugees from

What Can Be Done?

Syria, entered the EU, leading to tense domestic and international debates about 'how' migrants could be absorbed.

The migrant 'issue' is fuelling political change in several countries. In the UK, national politics is being transformed following the rise of the United Kingdom Independence Party (UKIP). This is focused on keeping 'foreigners' (mainland Europeans and others) from settling in the UK. In the once famously tolerant Netherlands the anti-immigration Party for Freedom (VVD), Geert Wilders' populist anti-Islam party, has become a partner in recent government coalitions. In Australia the government is using its foreign aid budget to pay poor Pacific Island countries to provide detention facilities for migrants who arrive in the country without visas, despite concerns that this breaches UN human rights treaties. There are many other examples: in Hungary, in Croatia, in Turkey, in Sweden – the list gets longer. Across the rich nations political parties with anti-immigrant manifestoes are doing very well. Foreign migrants, and especially those with darker skins, increasingly face a hostile reception.

Rich nations have been enthusiastic to open up global markets for goods, services and finance. The labour market, however, is the one market they are keen not to liberalize. But the vast wage differentials between rich and poor countries mean that opening up the cross-border mobility of low-skill labour only moderately would raise the annual earnings of poor-country citizens by more than US$51 billion.[10] Much of this would flow 'back home' as remittances. If you want to promote growth and reduce poverty in poor countries, then international migration is a win-win policy.

As a concrete example, take Bangladesh. The country's poverty problems (deep poverty in a land-constrained country that will suffer greatly from climate change) could be solved at a stroke with increased emigration: greater remittances, increased economic growth, improved public services and reduced environmental pressures (due to out-migration). Bangladesh has around 3% of its population living abroad. If this were to be increased to 10% of the population, the remittances generated would rise to well in excess of US$40 billion. This represents 2,624% of Bangladesh's annual aid flows. Moreover, if the multiplier effect of this extra income is included, the increased national income is estimated to be around US$84 billion – more than Bangladesh's GNI.[11] No wonder Branko Milanovic has declared that 'migration is probably the most powerful tool for reducing global poverty and inequality'.[12]

What Can Be Done?

There are two main ways in which migrants are a strategic tool for national development. The first is through remittances that lift relatives, their neighbours and communities out of poverty. According to the World Bank, remittances sent to developing countries topped US$436 billion in 2014. In some countries they compete as a source of income with exports. For example, in Pakistan in 2012, US$14 billion in remittances far surpassed its US$5 billion in cotton exports. Remittances are not only big but are also a stabilizing source of income when there are global financial crises. National governments can reap the benefits of remittances by building them into national development plans, as is increasingly being done.

The second beneficial mechanism is the ways in which the diaspora (i.e. migrants and their descendants) can engage in processes of development 'back home'. A country's diaspora can be an important source of business contacts, investment and technology and skills transfer. They can become a 'brain gain' rather than a 'brain drain'. India has energetically sought to harness its diaspora for national development. The rapid advance of the country's highly successful software and IT industries was fostered by the return of technical specialists and entrepreneurs from Silicon Valley. They brought 'home' finance to set up businesses and technological and management skills. This allowed them to establish world-beating businesses employing low-cost Indian labour with high-level skills.

But harnessing migration for national development faces serious challenges. These include the reluctance of rich nations to accept labour migrants, the rise of anti-migrant political parties and the lack of protection of migrants' labour rights. Despite the existence of global International Labour Organization Conventions for migrant workers, many are very low-paid and work in conditions that are not legally permitted in their countries of residence. In the Gulf region, especially in Qatar, migrant workers on construction projects have alarmingly high death rates from avoidable accidents. Some migrants are 'modern slaves', especially in agriculture and the sex industry in the US and Europe. The tough deportation practices operated by the EU mean that migrants 'without papers' have incentives to comply with traffickers.

The big picture

If rich nations are serious about helping the world's poor, then they need to focus on the issues that could make a big difference to poor people: fostering national development strategies that are genuinely owned by developing countries rather than imposed by the IMF and the World Bank; ensuring that poor countries can access the finance they need for national development and stopping national elites and MNCs from stealing their resources; making the Doha trade round a genuine development round by granting poor countries unreciprocated trade deals; and gradually opening up rich-world labour markets to low-skilled labour.

Such initiatives would not only be 'good' for the poor. They would also be 'good' for rich nations: creating a more prosperous and stable world so sustainable growth becomes a possibility; creating the labour force that will be needed to care for Europe and Japan's (and soon China's) increasingly aged populations; raising the capacity of all governments to tax profitable MNCs operating in their countries; and making flows of migrants more predictable. There are other actions rich nations should pursue: greater investment in research and development for tropical diseases and agriculture; reducing criminal violence by helping to reform law enforcement and criminal justice agencies; regulating the flow of small arms and weapons to poorer countries and especially fragile states; and strategic military interventions to prevent further conflict, when they are feasible. But there are also new challenges that must be tackled. Prime amongst these are climate change and spiralling global inequality, to which we now turn.

4

Climate Change and Inequality

Poor people living in poor countries have seen considerable improvements in their prospects over the last 25 years. Their likelihood of escaping extreme poverty, living longer and reasonably healthy lives and not seeing their children die is greater today than at any time in human history. The support rich nations provide for them is, as we have seen, highly imperfect and sometimes counter-productive. But – by a combination of design and good luck – things have been getting better in most poor countries and for many poor people. Maybe rich nations just need to keep on doing what they have been doing. If only things were that easy; but they are not. Every major advance that humanity makes seems inevitably to generate new problems.

In the twenty-first century two of these 'problems of success' – climate change and spiralling inequality – loom very large and are already starting to limit human progress. The material foundation of humanity's improved living standards over the last two centuries has been and is being achieved by economic growth processes that are carbon profligate. This cannot continue as the world's climate is warming and a set of poverty-creating environmental changes are underway. Allied to climate change, the socio-economic underpinnings of contemporary capitalism are generating income and wealth inequalities on a previously unimaginable scale. When Credit Suisse, a Swiss bank specializing in managing the wealth of the super-rich, publishes a study (*World Wealth Report 2014*) warning about the problem of inequality, then everyone should get worried. One of Oxfam's recent estimates claims a staggering tipping point will be crossed in 2016: the richest 1% of humanity will own as much wealth as the remaining 99%.

Climate change: this changes everything

Many people in rich nations believe that climate change and its causes are a scientific theory: 'some scientists agree with it and others disagree'. This is wrong – dangerously wrong. Virtually all scientists agree that global warming is occurring and the vast majority think that human activity is a major contributor to this warming. Only a few dissenters, often closely linked to hydrocarbon corporations, think differently. The global authority on climate change is the UN's Intergovernmental Panel on Climate Change (IPCC). For its most recent report in 2014 – the *Fifth Assessment Report (AR5)* – the panel comprised more than 800 world-leading, independent scientists who voluntarily contributed to its analysis of all of the scientific literature on the topic.[1]

The *AR5* panel concluded that

> warming of the climate system is unequivocal, and since the 1950s, many of the observed changes are unprecedented over decades to millennia. The atmosphere and ocean have warmed, the amounts of snow and ice have diminished, sea level has risen and the concentrations of greenhouse gases have increased. ... It is *extremely likely* [90% to 100% probability] that human influence has been the dominant cause of the observed warming since the mid-20th century.[2]

Key amongst these anthropogenic causes are industrialization, construction, transport, deforestation, agriculture and livestock rearing: all fuelled by growing numbers of people and 'consumer' lifestyles.

Climate Change and Inequality

Between 1906 and 2005 the global average surface temperature is estimated to have increased by 0.74°C. Between 2005 and 2100 this temperature could rise by 4.8°C according to the upper end of *AR5* scenarios. An increase of 2°C is almost certain given the present trajectory for CO_2 production, regardless of whatever mitigation we achieve in the near future. This does not simply mean that everywhere in the world will be a little warmer. It means that the patterns of global atmospheric and ocean flows will change and with that many different elements of the climate. In some places global warming will mean temperatures drop – it is complicated. As Naomi Klein's book title spells out: *This Changes Everything.*[3]

The complex nature of climate change, and of its causes, has been exploited by oil companies and right-wing lobby groups to manipulate media coverage. As a result of this cleverly engineered public 'misunderstanding' of science, it is more difficult for politicians to take concerted action to tackle global warming in the US for fear of losing public support. The way US oil companies have covertly engaged in shaping the climate change debate was revealed in 2002 when a memo from ExxonMobil to President George W. Bush was leaked. The memo pushed for the US government to oust the chair of the IPCC,

Robert Watson, and have him replaced by Rajendra Pachauri, who was seen as more mild-mannered and more industry-friendly. Shortly after the memo was sent, Watson was ousted and Pachauri replaced him.[4]

Modelling some aspects of climate change is possible with a reasonable degree of confidence, but other changes are more difficult to predict as there are potentially catastrophic changes that will be triggered if hard-to-identify 'thresholds' are exceeded. Key amongst these is an accelerated melting of the Greenland Ice Sheet. This would rapidly raise sea levels, by metres rather than centimetres – goodbye Amsterdam – and block the warm water flows of the Gulf Stream to Western Europe.

Climate change will dramatically restructure agriculture and industry around the world. Some areas will become less agriculturally and industrially productive while others will prosper. The three most significant changes for human populations are likely to be: rises in sea level; changes in temperature and precipitation; and the increased frequency of extreme weather events. Rising sea levels will affect coastal settlements around the world, particularly those with large populations living in low-lying areas. In Bangladesh, for instance, it has been estimated that between 6 and 8 million people will be displaced by 2050. Changes in temperature and rainfall patterns will impact greatly on agriculture and health and seem likely to be especially negative in Africa and South Asia. More frequent and changing patterns of extreme climatic events, natural disasters such as cyclones, floods and droughts, will impact immediately on livelihoods and cause immense suffering, with deaths and the destruction of property. In the longer term they may mean that some presently heavily settled areas could become uninhabitable.

While the degrees of confidence around predicting the effects of climate change and the ensuing consequences for different parts of the world vary, most scenarios indicate that poor people and poor countries will suffer most. *AR5* finds that:

> Throughout the 21st century, climate change impacts are projected to slow down economic growth, make poverty-reduction more difficult, further erode food security, and prolong existing and create new poverty traps, the latter particularly in urban areas and emerging hotspots of hunger (medium confidence) ... climate-related hazards exacerbate other stressors, often with negative outcomes for livelihoods, especially for people living in poverty (high confidence).[5]

Climate Change and Inequality

There are two main reasons why climate change will hurt the poor most. The first relates to pre-existing patterns of wealth. Poorer people and nations have fewer resources to devote to adapting to climate change (such as building embankments and raising electricity generators) and to invest in research and development on adaptation. The second is geographical: all of the IPCC scenarios suggest that the parts of the world with the highest concentrations of poverty – sub-Saharan Africa and South Asia – will experience a greater share of the negative consequences of climate change than will the middle- to high-latitude regions (Europe, North America and Japan). What will this mean?

Climate change is predicted to lead to an aggregate reduction in agricultural productivity sufficient to raise agricultural produce prices by between 2% and 20% over the short to medium term.[6] This automatically impacts most on the poor and poorest as they spend a greater share of their income on food. But it gets worse. The negative impacts are likely to be concentrated in rain-fed agriculture and in tropical regions. In parts of South Asia the prediction is that cereal yields could be down by 30% by 2050. For example, growing wheat in Bangladesh is likely to have become impossible by then. Even more dramatically, in Chad, Ethiopia, Nigeria,

Somalia, Sudan and Zimbabwe it is possible that growing cereal crops will be non-viable by 2080. Unless there are vast technological breakthroughs in agriculture, climate change seems certain to reduce both food security and economic growth in many of the world's poor countries.

Changes in rainfall patterns will lead to increased water stress (less than 1,000 cubic metres of reasonable-quality water per person per annum) and associated reductions in health, quality of life and economic opportunities. Estimates for Africa are of 75 to 250 million more people experiencing water stress between 2010 and 2020 and 350 to 600 million by 2050. Water stress will also increase greatly in Latin America and South Asia. Some military scenarios now warn of 'water wars' between ethnic groups in sub-Saharan Africa and between states in the Middle East and North Africa as water stress becomes extreme. Given the close association of violent conflict with poverty, this would be doubly problematic for the world's poor.

Rising sea levels and more frequent extreme weather events will mean that coastal regions experience higher levels of flooding, erosion and saline intrusion. A high proportion of the developing world's population is concentrated on the coast. These people are likely to experience both direct impacts on the quality of their lives and indirect impacts, through reduced economic prospects. A sea-rise increase of 40 cm would displace 13 to 94 million people in Asia. In Africa mega-cities are evolving on the coast – in 2015 there were three coastal cities of more than 8 million people as well as a cross-national megalopolis stretching from Accra to Port Harcourt of 50 million plus. Regular and severe flooding in low-lying areas, where poor people's shacks are concentrated, hampers social and economic progress and could lead to large-scale forced relocation. By 2050, several small island states in the Caribbean and the Pacific and Indian Oceans will be fully submerged and their entire populations displaced.

Climate change will also induce new patterns of morbidity and mortality. The overall balance seems likely to be negative, especially in tropical and near-tropical regions. Most predictions indicate that heat stress, malaria, Chagas disease, dengue fever, cholera and other water-borne diseases will increase. Higher temperatures and greater water stress raise the incidence of infections. Extreme events – cyclones, hurricanes, storm surges, floods and droughts – all impact negatively on health through drowning and injury, disease transmission and reduced resilience to health problems.

Specific predictions include greatly increased levels of dengue fever and larger numbers of heat stress-related deaths in China and India. In Africa the predictions are of increased diarrhoeal disease and cholera and an extension of the range for malaria and arboviruses (dengue, West Nile and other fevers). All of these problems will be compounded by food insecurity, as poor nutrition exacerbates the effects of disease, and by reduced access to health services, because of more frequent floods, power outages and other disruptions.

These negative consequences make the question 'What can be done?' a global priority. They have led to global poverty eradication and environmental sustainability being merged in the 2016–30 UN Sustainable Development Goals. Climate change reshapes thinking about tackling poverty in two particular ways. The first, and most obvious, is that the predicted impacts of climate change make the achievement of poverty reduction goals more difficult and more costly. The second is that anthropogenic climate change represents a fundamental challenge to thinking about economic development and social progress. The historically rapid improvements in the human condition since around 1820 have been closely associated with economic growth, and that growth has been based on the exploitation of non-renewable energy sources: coal, oil and gas. Contemporary economic growth is based on strategies that raise CO_2 concentrations in the atmosphere: energy-intensive industrialization, transportation and agriculture; deforestation; cattle-rearing; and energy-profligate lifestyles and consumption patterns. The recent prosperity of China and India has centred on industrialization and urbanization with associated rises in the use of hydrocarbons and destruction of forests.

Is it possible to reduce contemporary poverty without destroying the prospects of future generations? The glib answer to this is 'Yes, through a low-carbon economy and green growth'. This sounds very attractive, but ignores the fact that, despite recent investments in this area, such technologies are in their infancy. The wind farms of Europe, North America and (very recently) China may be a start, but the long-term energy plans of China, India, Indonesia, South Africa and now Japan are centred on massively increasing the use of coal (often dirty coal), gas and oil.

Climate Change and Inequality

Apocalypse soon?

So are we headed for global meltdown? Analysts identify two different approaches to reshaping the world's carbon-profligate development model: reformist and radical. The influential Stern Report of 2006 (*The Economics of Climate Change*) opted for reform, arguing from a social cost/benefit perspective that immediate and sharp reductions in greenhouse gases are needed. Delaying such reductions would mean that much greater costs would be incurred in the future in terms of reduced gross world product and/or the scale of investment needed to moderate the effects of climate change. Reformists view climate change as a consequence of a market failure: once this is corrected by charging for greenhouse gas emissions, then economic growth, and associated benefits for the rich and the poor, will continue, but in forms that are sustainable.

For radicals the Stern Report is nonsense: degrowth, not green growth, is required. Clive Spash writes: 'The [Stern Report] authors maintain allegiance to an economic orthodoxy which perpetuates the dominant political myth that traditional economic growth can be both sustained and answer all our problems.'[7] The extinction of species, the disappearance of glaciers, the flooding of coastal lands and climate-change-related human mortality represent losses which radicals believe cannot be valued by cost/benefit analysis. Many radicals adopt a rights-based analytical framework that rejects the market as a resource allocation system: 'Climate change, at least above a certain temperature rise, violates fundamental principles of sustainable development, intergenerational stewardship and fairness and therefore violates the inalienable rights of future generations.'[8] What is needed are: rapid reductions in consumption by the rich, so that CO_2 emissions dramatically fall; the adoption of low-consumption lifestyles around the world; and a global society that provides for itself from local production systems rather than international trade. 'Less is more.' A low-consumption lifestyle permits development that does not create environmental catastrophe, increases levels of personal satisfaction and fulfillment and re-connects humanity with nature in a spiritual sense.

At a less abstract level the debate about 'what to do' focuses on the ways in which *mitigation* (reducing CO_2 emissions so that climate change is not so rapid) and *adaptation* (changing present livelihoods so that people can better cope with climate change) form the basis for decision making. These analyses produce heated disagreements once questions are asked about who should mitigate (i.e. reduce) their production of greenhouse gases and who should pay for the costs of adaptation. Negotiations around these questions are always fraught, as shown by the refusal by the US to sign up to the Kyoto Protocol in the 1990s and the failures of the 2007 Bali Climate Summit, the 2009 Copenhagen Climate Summit and the 2012 Doha Climate Change Conference.

Fortunately the COP 21 Climate Summit in December 2015 appears to have broken through the impasse. With US and Chinese leadership, it managed to win the support of the UN's 195 member states for the Paris Agreement. This aims to achieve a zero net anthropogenic greenhouse gas emission level during the second half of the twenty-first century; strive towards global warming not exceeding 1.5°C (which would mean zero net emissions before 2050); and have five-yearly stakeholder reviews of national contributions towards a low-carbon global economy. The mechanisms are non-binding, with countries setting their own national targets for reductions and the stakeholder summits only 'naming and shaming' poorly performing countries. There would not be an international compliance process. While world leaders proclaimed this a great success, there was criticism and concern from civil society groups. If achieved, the national contributions pledged at Paris would limit global warming to an estimated 2.7°C. This is well above the 2°C international guideline, so contributions must be increased in the future, and these are only 'promises' not binding commitments. For radicals, Paris was a sell-out: charting a weak, reformist strategy that accepts species extinction and profound environmental degradation as inevitable.

My personal view is that the Paris Agreement provides grounds for optimism, albeit cautious optimism. The idea of climate justice that underpins parts of the Agreement provides a potential means of resolving the stumbling block of how much different nations should contribute to mitigation and adaptation costs. The Stockholm Environmental Institute's 'greenhouse development rights framework' illustrates this idea. If all individuals with an income above US$20 a day are viewed as being responsible for global warming (the higher your income, the more greenhouse gases you produce), and if one quantifies CO_2 emissions from 1990 (when global warming was first identified), then equitable 'national obligations' to mitigate and to fund adaptation policies can be computed. On this basis the US would take on 33.1% of global mitigation targets, the EU 25.7%, China 5.5% and India

0.5%. All countries would contribute to mitigation, but the least developed countries, with 12% of the world's population, would be responsible for only 0.01% of mitigation targets as they have emitted so little CO_2. If emerging powers such as China and India significantly increased their contributions to emissions in coming years, then their share of contributions could be increased by a set of common principles that apply to all nations.

The potential advantages of integrating the goals of tackling climate change with poverty eradication have been recognized at the UN and partly explain why the Millennium Development Goals (2000–15) converted into the UN Sustainable Development Goals (2016–30). As global warming seems likely to stay higher up the international agenda than global poverty (because it impacts much more directly on the material and cultural interests of powerful countries, major corporations and better-off people), it may be tactically most effective to promote policies for helping the poor through agreements associated with sustainability. This would include: increased funding for tropical agricultural research and health problems; constructing urban flood infrastructure; introducing global taxes or markets for carbon; and transferring low-carbon energy technologies to developing countries without patent charges. All of these policies would help mitigate climate change and assist poor people to adapt to such change, while directly reducing poverty.

But can policies to avoid the adverse consequences of global warming that involve regulating the production and consumption patterns of the world's richest nations and wealthiest people make progress in an increasingly unequal world?

Inequality – the rich keep getting richer

Inequality is a subject over which there has been great contention, but, very recently and unexpectedly, positions have begun to become more consensual. Historically, the contention arises when asking whether economic inequality is a bad or a good thing. It gets really heated when asking whether governments should do something about it. Hysteria then sometimes ensues when 'redistribution' is mentioned.

Those inclined to the Left will argue that intrinsically inequality is bad for humanity – it is unjust – and instrumentally it leads to negative outcomes for society as a whole. It may come as a surprise to some people but both the poor *and* the rich suffer from the wrongs of inequality. As

Richard Wilkinson and Kate Pickett have shown in *The Spirit Level*, in virtually every aspect of life (physical and mental health, education, decent work and even life satisfaction) rising inequality in rich nations is associated with lower levels of social indicators.[9] Those inclined to the Right will refute such arguments. Economists will cite Arthur Okun, whose book *Equality and Efficiency: The Big Tradeoff* persuaded many (especially in the US) that efforts to reduce inequality lead to reductions in efficiency that constrain enterprise and economic growth.[10] Such ideas informed leaders such as Reagan and Thatcher and fed the belief that 'greed is good'. Inequality, it was argued, spurs people to make greater efforts and fuels competition. These claims still appeal to the Republican Party in the US and parts of the UK Conservative Party.

But times have changed. It is not only heterodox economists and Left-leaning NGOs who declaim inequality. The IMF and, as we have seen, Credit Suisse have published authoritative studies that warn of the consequences of rising wealth inequality and the potential benefits of redistributive policies. Indeed, at the World Economic Forum in 2015 the world's wealthiest and most powerful people witnessed the heads of the IMF and the World Bank bemoaning the problems created by rising inequality.

Climate Change and Inequality

By any standards, inequality within nations is rising at spectacular rates. While different measures (wealth or income), different datasets (national accounts or taxation) and different analysts disagree on the detail, they all agree that the wealthiest are getting richer faster than anyone else (except in Latin America). The real income of the global top 1% rose by more than 60% between 1988 and 2008. And while there have been challenges to Oxfam's claim, noted above, that by 2016 the wealth of the top 1% will equal that of the remaining 99%, that tipping point will soon be reached if present trends continue. *Forbes Magazine* rated Bill Gates the world's richest person in 2014 with assets of US$79 billion. He displaced Mexico's Carlos Slim, who was worth only US$70 billion. Both of them had more wealth than the entire population of Uganda produces in a year (around US$50 billion). But Uganda was not left out of the super-rich listings: its wealthiest businessman, Sudhir Ruparelia, has entered the bottom ranks of Forbes *World's Billionaires* list. Overall the number of billionaires was up 15% from 2013 to 2014 – 268 new US$ billionaires in one year. But not all billionaires are saying that inequality is a good thing. Warren Buffett, the world's most successful investor, has pointed out that the share of income tax he paid the US Internal Revenue Service was lower than the clerical staff in his office: 'How can this be right? ... There's class warfare, all right ... but it's my class, the rich class, that's making war and we're winning.'[11]

The reasons for such growth in inequality are complex, but two factors stand out. First, contemporary capitalism is based on economic processes that permit those who manage to amass money by their brain power (Bill Gates), or political connections (Carlos Slim), or both (once you have the money, then the political connections soon follow), to increase their wealth faster than others. As Thomas Piketty tells us, the returns to capital (owning physical and financial assets) are greater than the returns to labour (working), as is the historical record for all but a part of the twentieth century.[12] So the rich get richer.

But there is also a political-economic reason. Those with excessive wealth are able to shape national and international public policies so much that they can ensure that they get wealthier. Their lobbying (look at the US), and perhaps less legitimate means of determining policy, permits 'regulatory capture' by plutocrats and oligarchs. They can ensure that national and international patent and competition laws allow them to dominate the markets in which they operate and that taxation laws allow them to avoid paying tax. By gaining control of the media, plutocrats can even persuade the public that inequality is good for everyone.

Nobel Prize-winner Joseph Stiglitz has written passionately about the ways in which inequality is eroding not just the fabric of the US economy but also the foundations of its political system. In *The Price of Inequality* he sees America as being 'of the 1%, for the 1%, by the 1%'.[13] The country's markets are not working, so inefficiency and instability have become economic norms. The political system has proved itself unable to correct such market failures, as it has aligned itself with the 1% – who benefit most from the country's inefficient and unstable markets. And, as a result, the economic and political systems have become 'fundamentally unfair' – they now accept that economic opportunity should not be open to all. Worse still, they ensure that social mobility (the potential for hard-working and high-achieving poorer people to become wealthy) has become an historical myth. Moreover, what happens in the US impacts on capitalism around the world. In Europe, Asia and Africa economic systems that are 'fundamentally unfair' are encouraged and, in turn, these foster highly unequal political systems.[14] For Stiglitz there is one underpinning factor that explains the Occupy movement in the US and Europe, the Arab Spring, turmoil in Greece, thousands of riots each year in rural China, and street protests in South Africa's cities: inequality.

The consequences of increasing inequality for economic growth and human welfare used to be highly debated, but now arguments are converging. You can anticipate that Oxfam will have negative findings about inequality. But, as noted above, the IMF has recently, and more surprisingly, come to a similar position, with its researchers concluding that

> it would still be a mistake to focus on growth and let inequality take care of itself, not only because inequality may be ethically undesirable but also because the resulting growth may be low and unstable ... redistribution, and the associate reduction in inequality, is thus associated with higher and more durable growth.

The IMF identifies a 'tentative consensus ... that inequality can undermine progress in health and education, cause investment-reducing political and economic instability, and undercut the social consensus required to adjust in the face of shocks ... it tends to reduce the pace and durability of growth'.[15]

So high levels of inequality raise the likelihood of growth collapsing, undermine education and health and exacerbate income poverty – but still it seems virtually impossible to tackle the issue!

What can be done? The revolutionary solution – seizing and redistributing land and assets – has few supporters following the collapse of communism and socialism. More reformist measures – taxation and fiscal redistribution through public expenditure in pro-poor education, health services and social protection – are gaining support. At the aggregate level Peter Lindert's seminal book *Growing Public* has demonstrated the ways in which rising social spending was associated with long-term economic growth and welfare improvements throughout the nineteenth and twentieth centuries.[16] At the national level, and in poorer countries, the recent evidence is clear that effective public expenditure on domestically financed education, health and social protection raises the prospects for sustained growth, structural transformation and welfare advances. Social policy is not simply about helping the poor and disadvantaged whilst incurring public 'costs'. It is about redistributing wealth into services that are public investments in creating sustained national economic growth, social cohesion and improved welfare for all citizens.

While the evidence for such policies is clear, enacting them in the places they are most needed – poor and very poor countries – is very problematic. The nature of many domestic business and political elites – greedy, extractive and predatory – allied to international business elites and the social norms they transmit ('make as much as you can as fast as you can . . . everyone is only in this for themselves'), means that socially beneficial policies are not effectively implemented. Progressive social policies are increasingly enacted in poorer countries, but the funding is lower than promised and/or service delivery institutions are not sanctioned for their failure to provide poor people with basic services.

The strength of the domestic business lobby in many poorer countries – allied to the opening up of economies so that multinational businesses can transfer misprice products to avoid taxation or threaten to 'leave' a country if they are taxed more than they like – often restrains the capacity of poorer countries to finance social spending. Weaknesses in governance – sometimes owing to a lack of capacity, but sometimes also the result of the more pernicious and active mismanagement of public resources (as in Afghanistan) – means that in many parts of the world public services (education, health and social protection) are not delivered in ways that will enhance welfare and underpin future growth – and businesses and wealthy people are able to avoid their taxation and revenue obligations.

The power of the '1%' may appear unassailable. Will we have to wait for a miracle for this to change – such as Bill Gates admitting that his mega-philanthropy will not eradicate global poverty? That businesses and entrepreneurs (like him) need to be regulated in ways that ensure they do not undermine domestic revenue mobilization? That they need to contribute more to public expenditure so that governments can promote broad-based growth, prosperity for all and welfare, and so that plutocracy can be replaced by democracy? Or will a growing tide of protest and its consequences – sometimes socially progressive, and sometimes regressive, as in Egypt – be needed to persuade the 1% that they will not get the world they want for their grandchildren if they continue to promote inequality as a global social norm?

Escaping dystopia

Perhaps the contemporary popularity of movies set in dystopian futures of global environmental and social collapse – *Avatar*, *The Hunger Games*, *In*

Climate Change and Inequality

Time, *The Road*, *Mad Max*, the *Divergent* series
and others – is just a fad. Alternatively, could
it be a sign of the rising feeling that 'things' are
slipping out of control, and that the leaders of
rich nations are unwilling or unable to improve
the human security of their citizens? The direct
responsibility of rich nations for the growing concentrations of greenhouse gases creates a moral
requirement for them both to reduce emissions
and to compensate poorer people for the damage
that is being/will be caused. Alongside this environmental challenge is the challenge arising from
the present wave of global capitalism. This wave
has successfully reduced extreme poverty but it is
driving up economic inequality in most countries at
an unprecedented rate. A narrow elite of plutocrats
(the 1%, or perhaps more accurately the 0.1%) can
increasingly determine national and international
policies and shape public opinion through their
control of the media.

The emerging problems faced by humanity
– climate change and inequality – allied to the
continuing problems of the past – including foreign
aid that is at best only partially effective; an unfair
international trade regime; policy imposition by the
World Bank and the IMF; lack of access to finance
for development; and, barriers to migration – create

an imperative (both moral and self-interested) for rich nations to provide more effective support to poor people and poor countries. What forms could such action take? How might it be actively fostered?

5

From Broken Promises to Global Partnership

Rich nations, and their citizens, should do much more to help the world's poor people. They need to do this for two reasons. First, ethically it is the right thing to do. Second, it is in their self-interest. On a small, densely populated, highly connected planet a problem in a faraway place can soon create difficulties for rich nations – whether that is unexpected migration, new health dangers, increased flows of narcotics, threats to national security or other problems. It is time to move on from the broken promises of the past to forging a genuine global partnership for all of humanity to have the prospects for a decent life.

A relatively easy first step in strengthening this partnership is augmenting steadily the foreign aid spending of the global laggards – Japan, South Korea and the US – and greatly improving aid effectiveness of all donor agencies. But this is only a first step. It would not transform the rates at which poor people can improve their lives. To make real progress, rich nations must focus on the big picture: the policy issues that could drive forward growth, sustainability and equity. And they, or perhaps more accurately their concerned citizens in partnership with concerned citizens in poorer countries, will need to engage with the international political economy of development. The vested interests that support 'business as usual' have to be tackled. Making a difference – creating more effective local, national and global partnerships for inclusive development – means thinking through what needs to be done and taking political action.

What needs to be done?

There are five main policy domains that must be re-engineered. First, the policy space for poor countries to design nationally owned strategies for job-creating growth and improved human development – better health, education and social cohesion – must be expanded. Such policies have to be sound in terms of macroeconomic stability, but could incorporate industrial policies fostering infant industries, and redistributive social policies providing quality education, basic health services and social protection for the more vulnerable. Taking the Washington Consensus medicine produced only limited results in many low-income countries. The big successes – the original Asian Tigers, China, India, Malaysia, Mauritius, Vietnam and others – have been based on more heterodox strategies that were nationally owned.

Second, major reforms to international finance could significantly increase the flow of finance for development and dramatically reduce illicit and illegal flows of capital out of poorer countries by multinational businesses and national elites. Flows of development finance are already transforming as Chinese bilateral finance and Chinese-led multilateralism become more important. Alongside these flows, BRICS initiatives are increasing the availability of finance. Multinationals are coming under increased surveillance as rich countries have realized that it is not just poor countries that are being ripped off through tax avoidance.

Third, international trade negotiators need to keep the promises that were made in 2000 for a 'development round' that would genuinely level the playing field for poor countries based on a series of non-reciprocated agreements. The UN Sustainable

Development Goals reaffirm the need for this, particularly on trade in agricultural products. Alongside trade, international migration will have to be included within negotiations about economic liberalization – liberalizing global flows of capital, goods and services has to be linked to liberalizing labour flows. This would be good for the poor, but it is also essential for maintaining economic growth and social welfare in rapidly ageing parts of the world: Europe, Japan and, soon, China. While no rich nation will be prepared to fully open its labour market, it is essential to honour existing refugee treaties and manage migration more effectively than contemporary 'Fortress Europe' (and 'Fortress Australia') policies are doing.

Fourth, if humanity is to have a secure and equitable future, climate change must be addressed. The carbon emissions of the industrialized world's energy-profligate citizens and businesses over the last two centuries have created the problem of global warming. As a result, the rich nations must take the lead in mitigating carbon emissions and paying for countries to adapt to a changed climate (rising sea levels, more unpredictable and more extreme temperature and rainfall patterns and increased numbers of climate-related disasters). But economic growth in the BRICs and other emerging economies now means that many middle-income countries are increasing their greenhouse gas emissions. They will need to take action. The progress made with the Paris Agreement of 2015, approved by all 195 UN member states, creates a basis for cautious optimism about the prospects for capping greenhouse gas emissions and financing climate change adaptation.

The last, but definitely not the least, problem that needs to be tackled is the spiralling income and wealth inequality produced by contemporary global capitalism. All of the big issues that must be addressed if rich nations are to genuinely help the world's poor and create a viable future for their own citizens are undermined by the acceptance of high levels of inequality between and within nations. Capitalism has returned to its historic norm: concentrating wealth in the hands of a small part of the population that controls capital (physical, financial and intellectual assets). Even more alarming is Joseph Stiglitz's evidence that rising economic inequality is undermining democracy. As noted above, relatively small group of plutocrats – the 1% or perhaps the 0.1% – are increasingly able to shape national and international policies because of their capacity to (i) control national political debates in their 'home' countries, and (ii) shape international negotiations between countries. By sheltering behind corporate social responsibility programmes, philanthropic trusts and media appearances alongside celebrities, these elites are able to partially disguise their predatory social norms and behaviour.

Making change happen

Rich nations have an increasing understanding of 'what' could be done to create an equitable and viable future for all of humanity. The real crunch comes not when asking 'What should be done?' but when asking 'How can change happen?' Our leaders are good at making grand statements about helping the poor and saving the global environment – from Rio (1992 and 2012) to New York (2000 and 2015) – but they are not so good at honouring these commitments. Nor are we, the citizens of 'post-democratic' rich nations (increasingly disillusioned with our political leaders and parties), as effective as we could be at demanding that our leaders keep their promises. How can the vested interests that benefit from injustice, inequality and environmental degradation be challenged? This requires thinking strategically, thinking organizationally, thinking tactically and taking action.

Strategically, progress has to be made in terms of ideas and organization. An all-out war of ideas is needed in the public sphere to raise the understanding of the reasons why rich nations should help poor people and poor countries and put real pressure on political leaders to do things differently. This war of ideas will have to explain the ethical grounds for supporting the poor and the more self-interested reasons: creating an economically, socially and environmentally sustainable context for the prosperity of the citizens of rich nations. While there are many detailed ideas that will need promoting – aid effectiveness, access to medicines for the poor, managing the liberalization of labour flows, climate justice, inclusive growth, fertility rates lowered through prosperity, reduced economic inequality, and many more – the over-arching principles that have to be pursued must be clear. We live in 'one world', and if we want good lives for ourselves and prospects for good lives for our children and future generations, then social justice (reduced poverty and inequality) and environmental sustainability must be actively pursued.

Organizationally, there are great challenges. While developmental NGOs in rich nations have made considerable progress in campaigning and advocacy at elite levels, they have increasingly become disconnected from their civil societies. Their professionally mounted campaigns, superb reports and persuasive PowerPoint presentations can challenge and help reshape debates in national assemblies and international meetings. But these successes are rarely converted into mobilized civic action or changed public attitudes comparable to earlier efforts such as Jubilee 2000 and fair trade. NGOs, whether big-brand or small-scale, need to reconnect with their supporters – donations are not enough. Supporters need to be encouraged to behave more like members and take forward ideas and concerns themselves – with neighbours, councillors, representatives and MPs, and political parties. Campaigning cannot just be left to the professionals and focus groups: to make progress it needs to have social roots – in churches and mosques, student societies, trade unions, women's institutes, farmer associations, consumer societies. Out of such roots, coalitions can emerge to create a civic voice and mobilize political action. Given the inclusive goals of global development, these coalitions must seek to operate at multiple scales and connect people and organizations across rich and poor nations. This is difficult, but the examples of the women's movement, fair trade movement, Shack Dwellers International and others show that NGOs and civil society groups can create innovative and effective organizational forms. In a world where vested interests are well organized, those working for social change have to get organized themselves.

Tactically, two very different paths for citizens, civil society groups, NGOs and coalitions of the concerned can be identified. First is a concerted push for radical change in the policies and practices of rich nations. What forms might these take? At the modest end comes the Jubilee 2000 movement, forming a human chain around the G8 meeting of 1998 in Birmingham (UK) to demand that highly indebted poor countries are forgiven their debt – billions in debt was subsequently written off. More assertive is the Occupy movement in 2008 and 2009 seizing the streets in London, New York and elsewhere. More aggressive and more controversial are the protesters at the 1999 WTO meeting in Seattle, whose violence closed the city down for a day but opened the doors for much fuller NGO and civil society engagement in trade negotiations. This helped push the WTO into declaring Doha a development round.

But the tactics used at Seattle went well beyond civil disobedience and involved physical violence against property and the police. I remember discussing this with senior Oxfam staff the day after the riots, one of whom said: 'Oxfam would never support the use of violence. But we are not dissatisfied with the results of the protests. Within hours, doors that had always been closed to us were opened.' As a point of principle, development organizations cannot adopt violent or direct action approaches as that would abrogate the values they are promoting: democratic negotiations, listening to others and human rights. The tactics to achieve a socially just world do not make rapid advances easy.

And so to the second approach of gradualist reform: accepting that episodic, evolutionary processes of change may be 'as good as it gets' and seeking to maximize the opportunity for such episodes. These include the sorts of gradual, progressive change that have been happening over many years: slowly improving aid effectiveness for some donors; the recognition of the need for a developmental trade round; and the acceptance by rich nations of 'common but differentiated responsibilities' for climate change. These changes are incremental, but they add up to improved prospects for the poor of the world. With the continuing restructuring of the global economy, shifting towards Asia, there is a possibility of change episodes accelerating – as has happened with finance for development.

But perhaps the radical and evolutionary

approaches to promoting progressive social change are best understood not as an 'either/or' choice. Combinations of strategy are needed involving formal and often informal networks of organizations and individuals. Radical and campaigning civil society organizations that confront vested interests can open up political space for reformist groups to negotiate policy change. As a result those seeking to advance the interest of the world's poor need to view their activities from a network perspective. The campaigning organization with its (literally) killer argument 'Nestlé kills babies' opens the door for advocacy organizations and professional researchers to negotiate specific changes in company policies. Demanding radical change can accelerate more incremental processes of progressive change.

The shift to a multipolar world has created, and continues to create, new political space that could be shaped into opportunities for progressive change. The competition that rich nations now face from the rising powers, especially China and Brazil, and emerging middle powers may mean that they have to try to do better with their soft power tools (aid, a willingness to take a lead on tackling major problems, contributing to global public goods) to maintain their international standing and legitimacy. Goal 8 of the Millennium Development Goals promised 'global partnership' but this never really became established. It is impossible to predict whether the changed international political economy of the late 2010s, alongside re-energized national agency – Brazil taking a leading role on sustainability; China and the US collaborating on limiting CO_2 emissions; the UK providing leadership for bilateral aid agencies; perhaps Russia finding that cooperation is the way to make progress in the face of a common enemy (Daesh) – will produce a more positive outcome than the 'Millennium Moment'. Regardless, the shift from the Millennium Development Goals to the Sustainable Development Goals and the pressing need to reach agreement on greenhouse gas emissions has created new windows of opportunity.

Moving faster towards 'one world'

For the poor of the world the 'metrics' indicate that things have been getting better and at an increased rate in recent times. But still, depending on how you do the sums, between 1 billion and 3 billion people live in poverty: deprived of at least one of their most basic human needs. The pace of improvement in the well-being of these billions is too slow, given that we live in a materially, technologically and organizationally affluent world. The resources are available to provide all of humanity with their basic needs. Those resources are probably sufficient to even ensure a modestly decent standard of living (*buen vivir*) and reduced vulnerability for all of humanity. But the leaders of rich nations cannot find the commitment to reorganize the world in ways that will permit everyone to live a life with dignity and have prospects for achieving their aspirations.

Moving to an equitable, inclusive and sustainable world (what Peter Singer frames as recognizing that we are 'one world'[1]) will be a struggle. But there are very good reasons why the citizens and leaders of rich nations should take action, should take a lead. Some of these are ethically based. Rich nations have the capacity to help poorer countries and poor people improve their prospects. This ranges from making foreign aid more effective to negotiating for global policies and actions that help poor people advance themselves: fair trade, access to finance and technology, research on tropical diseases, and others. And rich nations are in part responsible for the present denial of opportunities to poor people, in terms of their histories of colonial and imperial exploitation, the forms of economic relations they have created and the way their carbon emissions have generated climate change. They have, at the very least, significantly caused these problems, so they have a moral duty to tackle them.

Beyond these ethical arguments comes the self-interested case. If the citizens of rich nations want a decent future for their children and grandchildren, then they have to create a fairer and more sustainable world. Continuing on the present path – unsustainable systems of production and consumption; high levels of preventable poverty; spiralling economic inequality; social and political exclusion – will not create the society they want. To attain a world in which there is a sustainable future for themselves and subsequent generations; economic, social and environmental stability; and personal and national security, rich nations have to help the poor much more effectively. Many of the policy changes and actions needed have been spelt out in this book. These have to be very different from earlier approaches. The rich nations have to move 'beyond aid' and systematically tackle the big issues for social justice: trade, climate change, migration, access to finance and technology and genuinely promoting social justice as a global social norm. This may seem unlikely, but so did abolishing slavery, winning votes for women, creating international humanitarian law and, most recently, reducing the share of humanity mired in extreme poverty from around 47% in 1990 to 14% in 2015. Achieving a socially just and sustainable world will not be easy, but it is possible to move in that direction much more quickly than we are.

Further Reading

Readers wanting to understand the history and contemporary nature of global development should start with Angus Deaton's *The Great Escape: Health, Wealth and the Origins of Inequality* (Princeton: Princeton University Press, 2013) for a superb analysis. Charles Kenny's *Getting Better: Why Global Development Is Succeeding and How We Can Improve the World Even More* (New York: Basic Books, 2011) provides an upbeat account of the human condition. My own book *Global Poverty: Global Governance and Poor People in the Post-2015 Era* (London: Routledge, 2015) examines the idea of global poverty and subsequently outlines theories of global development and practices of global poverty reduction. To understand the historical processes of state formation and inclusive governance that explain so much about prosperity and poverty read Daron Acemoglu and James Robinson's *Why Nations Fail: The Origins of Power, Prosperity and Poverty* (London: Profile Books, 2012).

For an exploration of the prospects of the world's poorest people, particularly in Africa, see Paul Collier's *The Bottom Billion: Why the Poorest Countries Are Failing and What Can be Done About It* (Oxford: Oxford University Press , 2007). However, Andy Sumner, in 'Where do the poor live?', *World Development* 40(5) (2012): 865–77, points out that the majority of the world's poor now live in middle-income countries, notably India and China. Datasets on human development and poverty are available at *www.worldbank.org*, *www.un.org* and *www.ophi.org.uk*, but be aware of how unreliable much of the data can be. Morten Jerven's *Poor Numbers: How We Are Misled by African Development Statistics and What to Do About It* (Ithaca, NY: Cornell University Press, 2013) explains in detail how statistics on poverty and development can undermine analysis and understanding. For annual assessments of what rich nations are doing for the global poor, look at the Commitment to Development Index at *www.cgdev. org*.

Good books on the ethics of helping poor

people are Peter Singer's *The Life You Can Save: Acting Now to End World Poverty* (New York: Picador, 2009), Thomas Pogge's *World Poverty and Human Rights* (Cambridge: Polity, 2008) and Dean Chatterjee's collection *The Ethics of Assistance: Morality and the Distant Needy* (Cambridge: Cambridge University Press, 2004). Peter Singer's 'Famine, affluence, and morality', *Philosophy and Public Affairs* 1(3) (1972): 229–43, is a ground-breaking essay that continues to have great relevance. In Dan Brockington's *Celebrity Advocacy and International Development* (London: Routledge, 2014) post-democratic theory is used to explain rich-nation public attitudes and apathy to development and poverty. The full theory is elaborated in Colin Crouch's *Post-Democracy* (Cambridge: Polity, 2004).

The literature on foreign aid, the focus of chapter 2, is vast. For a comprehensive assessment, see Roger Riddell's *Does Foreign Aid Really Work?* (Oxford: Oxford University Press, 2007). For a more recent assessment by a seasoned 'insider', look at Myles Wickstead's *Aid and Development: A Brief Introduction* (Oxford: Oxford University Press, 2015). The case that increased foreign aid can play a leading role in eradicating poverty is made in Jeffrey Sachs' *The End of Poverty: How We Can*

Make It Happen in Our Lifetime (London: Penguin, 2005). The counter-argument that aid has only a minor role and/or may cause poverty comes in two erudite books by William Easterly: *The White Man's Burden: Why the West's Efforts to Aid the Rest Have Done So Much Ill and So Little Good* (New York: Penguin Press, 2006) and *The Tyranny of Experts: Economists, Dictators and the Forgotten Rights of the Poor* (New York: Basic Books, 2013). For a deep understanding of how foreign aid programmes evolve in different countries, read Carol Lancaster's *Foreign Aid: Diplomacy, Development, Domestic Politics* (Chicago: University of Chicago Press, 2007). Emma Mawdsley's *From Recipients to Donors: Emerging Powers and the Changing Development Landscape* (London: Zed Press, 2012) explores how the BRICs have impacted on foreign aid. For a review of the role of NGOs in development, see my book with Michael Edwards, *Too Close for Comfort? NGOs, States and Donors* (London: Palgrave, second edition, 2014).

Moving to chapter 3, a thoughtful paper that persuasively argues that rich nations must go 'beyond aid' is Nancy Birdsall, Dani Rodrik and Arvind Subramanian's 'How to help poor countries', *Foreign Affairs* 84(4) (2005):136–52. Two excellent books by Dani Rodrik, *One Economics,*

Further Reading

Many Recipes: Globalization, Institutions and Economic Growth (Princeton: Princeton University Press, 2009) and *The Globalization Paradox: Why Global Markets, States and Democracy Can't Co-exist* (Oxford: Oxford University Press, 2012), explain how and why national policies, international trade and international finance constrain the progress of poor countries and poor people, and how the world might move towards a 'sane globalization'. Critical early explorations of these issues came from Ha-Joon Chang's *Kicking Away the Ladder: Development Strategy in Historical Perspective* (London: Anthem Press, 2002) and *Bad Samaritans: Rich Nations, Poor Policies and the Developing World* (London: Business Books, 2007). For a right-wing polemic on these issues, read Deepak Lal's *Poverty and Progress: Realities and Myths about Global Poverty* (Washington, DC: Cato Institute, 2013). For the left-wing counter-blast, see John Hilary's *The Poverty of Capitalism: Economic Meltdown and the Struggle for What Comes Next* (London: Pluto Press, 2013).

A fascinating proposal about how to escape the present impasse in trade negotiations comes from Rorden Wilkinson's *What's Wrong with the WTO and How to Fix It* (Cambridge: Polity, 2014). See Dev Kar, Raymond Baker and Tom Cardamore's

Further Reading

Illicit Financial Flows: The Most Damaging Economic Condition Facing the Developing World (Washington, DC: Global Financial Integrity, 2015) for an examination of how financial flows create poverty, and for data visit *www.gfintegrity.org*. Paul Collier's *Exodus: Immigration and Multiculturalism in the 21st Century* (London: Penguin, 2014) provides insights into the relationships between global poverty, inequality and mass international migration. Ian Goldin, Geoffrey Cameron and Meera Balarajan's *Exceptional People: How Migration Shaped Our World and Will Define Our Future* (Princeton: Princeton University Press, 2011) examines the past, present and future of migration. For the detailed case that rich nations, and particularly the US, could do a lot more to reduce violence and improve access to law enforcement and criminal justice in poor countries, read Gary Haugen and Victor Boutros' *The Locust Effect: Why the End of Poverty Requires the End of Violence* (New York: Oxford University Press, 2014). Christopher Coker's *Can War Be Eliminated?* (Cambridge: Polity, 2014) provides a scholarly assessment of the prospects for global peace – he is not optimistic.

The contemporary authoritative examinations of climate change and its impacts, one of the twin themes of chapter 4, are by the Intergovernmental

Panel on Climate Change (IPCC) and are known as the Fifth Assessment Report (*AR5*). There are four detailed reports published in 2013 and 2014, but often their summaries are more than sufficient. Reports are available from *www.ipcc.ch/report/ar5*. For an economic analysis read Nicholas Stern's *Why Are We Waiting? The Logic, Urgency and Promise of Tackling Climate Change* (Cambridge, MA: MIT Press, 2015). Naomi Klein, in *This Changes Everything: Capitalism vs The Climate* (London: Allen Lane, 2014), forcefully argues for dramatic and immediate action by everyone. For an absolutely opposite perspective – that climate change is not happening and we need do nothing – take a flip through Alan Moran's collection *Climate Change: The Facts* (London: Stockade Books, 2015).

The classic text for understanding the damaging effects of inequality, the other main theme of chapter 4, is Richard Wilkinson and Kate Pickett's *The Spirit Level: Why Equality Is Better for Everyone* (London: Penguin, 2010). For the US, see Joseph Stiglitz's *The Price of Inequality* (London: Penguin, 2013). Thomas Piketty, with his *Capital in the Twenty-First Century* (Cambridge, MA: Belknap Press, 2014), has put inequality at the top of the world's intellectual agenda, but at 685 pages his book is a challenge. Perhaps his colleague François

Further Reading

Bourguignon's *The Globalization of Inequality* (Princeton: Princeton University press, 2015) is more relevant for this book as he takes a global perspective to argue for 'fairer globalization'. An excellent and highly accessible read is Branko Milanovic's *The Haves and Have-Nots: A Brief and Idiosyncratic History of Global Inequality* (New York: Basic Books, 2011). Milanovic is the world's leading measurer of inequality, so do look at his *Global Inequality: A New Approach for the Age of Globalization* (Cambridge, MA: Harvard University Press, 2016).

Peter Singer's excellent *One World: The Ethics of Globalization* (New Haven: Yale University Press, 2002) summarizes the moral philosophy of equity and sustainability. In *The Age of Sustainable Development* (New York: Columbia University Press, 2015) Jeffrey Sachs tries to pull all the issues in this book together with an analytical theory that also provides an ethical framework for action. But watch out for his many critics. Finally, if you are looking for something on any detailed aspect of global development, go to the 52 specialist chapters in Bruce Currie-Alder, Ravi Kanbur, David Malone and Rohinton Medhora's *International Development: Ideas, Experience and Prospects* (Oxford: Oxford University Press, 2014).

Notes

Chapter 1 Why Worry About the Distant Poor?

1 Since late 2015 the World Bank's extreme poverty line has been US$1.90 a day at 2011 purchasing prices. Before that date this line was set at US$1.25 a day (2004 prices) and most sources use this as their poverty line. The original World Bank extreme poverty line of 2000 was US$1.08 a day and was called the 'dollar-a-day poverty line'.

2 For data on ODA, see the OECD's website (*www.oecd.org*).

3 For details and figures see *www.cgdev.org/article/commitment-development-index-cdi-2015-results*.

4 Peter Singer, 'Famine, affluence, and morality', *Philosophy and Public Affairs* 1(3) (1972): 231–2.

5 See *www.gfintegrity.org* for comprehensive reports and datasets.

6 See Kasper Lippert-Rasmussen, 'Global injustice and redistributive wars', *Law, Ethics and Philosophy* 1(1) (2013): 87–111.

7 I use the title 'Daesh' rather than 'Islamic State' as this organization is neither 'Islamic' nor a 'state'.

8 Wojciech Kopczuk, Joel Slemrod and Shlomo Yitzhaki, 'The limitations of decentralized world redistribution: an optimal taxation approach', *European Economic Review* 49(4) (2005): 1051–79.

9 Colin Crouch, *Post-Democracy* (Cambridge: Polity, 2004).

10 Angus Deaton, *The Great Escape: Health, Wealth and the Origins of Inequality* (Princeton: Princeton University Press, 2013).

11 Historically, commodity prices have tended to 'cycle' up and down. However, the recent rapid growth of the Chinese economy led to 15 years of soaring prices for producers of oil, copper, gold, iron and other commodities. This era has now ended.

12 Peace-building and conflict prevention could be added to this list, but these are vast topics dealt with in another volume in this series: Christopher Coker, *Can War Be Eliminated?* (Cambridge: Polity, 2014).

Chapter 2 The Limits of Foreign Aid

1 UN General Assembly Millennium Declaration 2000: 4.

2 A low-income country has average annual per capita income of less than US$1,045. A lower-middle-income country has per capita income between US$1,045 and US$4,125 per annum.

3 Carol Lancaster, *Foreign Aid: Diplomacy,*

Development, Domestic Politics (Chicago: University of Chicago Press, 2007).

4 William Easterly, *The White Man's Burden: Why the West's Efforts to Aid the Rest Have Done So Much Ill and So Little Good* (New York: Penguin Press, 2006), 4.

5 Dambisa Moyo, *Dead Aid: Why Aid Is Not Working and How There Is Another Way for Africa* (London: Penguin, 2010), 26.

6 'Dutch disease' posits that a rapid inflow of foreign currency into a country leads to an increased exchange rate and the marginalization of manufacturing and, perhaps, agriculture, and that this reduces economic growth.

7 A particular problem concerns causality. A positive relationship between aid and growth or aid and poverty reduction might occur because donors allocate aid to countries that are doing well. Conversely, a negative relationship may mean that donors are allocating aid where it is most needed: where there is low growth and desperate human need.

8 Deaton, *The Great Escape*, 288

9 Roger C. Riddell, *Does Foreign Aid Really Work?* (Oxford: Oxford University Press, 2007).

10 Nancy Birdsall, Dani Rodrik and Arvind Subramanian, 'How to help poor countries', *Foreign Affairs* 84(4) (2005): 136–52.

11 Charles Wolf, Jr, Xiao Wong and Eric Warner, *China's Foreign Aid and Government-Sponsored Investment Activities* (Santa Monica, CA: Rand Corporation, 2013).

12 Birdsdall et al., 'How to help poor countries', 136–7.
13 Daron Acemoglu and James Robinson, *Why Nations Fail: The Origins of Power, Prosperity and Poverty* (London: Profile Books, 2012).
14 Paul Collier, *The Bottom Billion: Why the Poorest Countries Are Failing and What Can be Done About It* (Oxford: Oxford University Press, 2007), 123.

Chapter 3 What Can Be Done?

1 This is taken from William Easterly's book: *The Elusive Quest for Growth: Economists' Adventures and Misadventures in the Tropics* (Cambridge, MA: MIT Press, 2001).
2 Ha-Joon Chang, *Bad Samaritans: Rich Nations, Poor Policies and the Developing World* (London: Business Books, 2007).
3 Angus Deaton et al., *An Evaluation of World Bank Research, 1998–2005* (Washington, DC: World Bank, 2006), 53.
4 Alexander Kentikelenis, Lawrence King, Martin McKee and David Stuckler, 'The International Monetary Fund and the Ebola outbreak', *The Lancet Global Health* 3(2) (2015): e69–e70.
5 Robert H. Wade, 'What strategies are viable for developing countries today? The World Trade Organization and the shrinking of "development space"', *Review of International Political Economy* 10(4) (2003): 621–44, 622.
6 Shawn Donnan, 'WTO plunged into crisis as doubts grow over its future', *Financial Times*, 1 August 2014.

7 Jagdish N. Bhagwati, *Termites in the Trading System: How Preferential Agreements Undermine Free Trade* (New York: Oxford University Press, 2008), 63.

8 See the Fair Trade Foundation (*www.fairtrade. org.uk*), Oxfam (*www.maketradefair.org.uk*) and Cafédirect (*www.cafedirect.co.uk*).

9 Martin Wolf, *Why Globalization Works* (New Haven, CT: Yale University Press, 2004), 206.

10 Terrie Walmsley and Alan Winters, 'Relaxing the restrictions on the temporary movement of natural persons: a simulation analysis', *Journal of Economic Integration* 20(4) (2005): 688–726.

11 Jonathon W. Moses, 'Leaving poverty behind: a radical proposal for developing Bangladesh', *Development Policy Review* 27(4) (2009): 457–79.

12 Branko Milanovic, *Global Inequality: From Class to Location, from Proletarians to Migrants* (World Bank Policy Research Working Paper, September 2011).

Chapter 4 Climate Change and Inequality

1 The IPCC publishes assessment reports every five to seven years. Its *AR5* is comprised of four documents published between September 2013 and November 2014. The best starting point is IPCC, *Climate Change 2014: Synthesis Report* (Geneva: IPCC, 2014). All reports and updates are available at *www. ipcc.ch*.

2 IPCC, *Climate Change 2013: The Physical Science Basis*, available at *www.ipcc.ch* (italics in original).

3 Naomi Klein, *This Changes Everything: Capitalism vs the Climate* (London: Allen Lane, 2014).

4 Fred Pearce, 'Top climate scientist ousted', *New Scientist*, 19 April 2002, and Julian Borger, 'US oil lobby oust climate change scientist', *Guardian*, 20 April 2002.

5 IPCC, *Climate Change 2014: Impact, Adaptation and Vulnerability*, available at *www.ipcc.ch*.

6 Data from IPCC *AR5* Reports and Lael Brainard, Abigail Jones and Nigel Purvis, *Climate Change and Global Poverty* (Washington, DC: Brookings Institution, 2009).

7 Clive Spash, 'The economics of climate change impacts à la Stern: novel and nuanced or rhetorically restricted?', *Ecological Economics* 63(4) (2007): 706–13, 706.

8 Eric Neumayer, 'A missed opportunity: the Stern Review on climate change fails to tackle the issue of non-substitutable loss of natural capital,' *Global Environmental Change* 17(3) (2007): 297–301, 297.

9 Richard Wilkinson and Kate Pickett, *The Spirit Level: Why Equality is Better for Everyone* (London: Penguin, 2010).

10 Arthur M. Okun, *Equality and Efficiency: The Big Tradeoff* (Washington, DC: Brookings Institution, 1975).

11 Ben Stein, 'In class warfare, guess which class is winning', *New York Times*, 26 October 2006.

12 Thomas Piketty, *Capital in the Twenty-First Century* (Cambridge, MA: Belknap Press, 2014).

13 Joseph Stiglitz, *The Price of Inequality* (London: Penguin, 2013), xi.
14 The one part of the world that is bucking this trend is Latin America. Income inequality was at very high levels in this region but has been reducing in most countries since 2000.
15 Jonathan Ostry, Andrew Berg and Charambos Tsangarides, *Redistribution, Inequality and Growth* (Washington, DC: International Monetary Fund, 2014), pp. 25, 4.
16 Peter H Lindert, *Growing Public: Social Spending and Economic Growth since the Eighteenth Century*, Vols 1 and 2 (Cambridge: Cambridge University Press, 2004).

Chapter 5 From Broken Promises to Global Partnership

1 Peter Singer, *One World: The Ethics of Globalization* (New Haven: Yale University Press, 2002).